HOW TO WRITE THAT SCENE

by Rayne Hall

HOW TO WRITE THAT SCENE

by Rayne Hall

Book cover by Erica Syverson and Manuel Berbin

© 2018 Rayne Hall

April 2018 Edition

ISBN-13: 978-1986958080

ISBN-10: 1986958086

British English.

TABLE OF CONTENTS

INTRODUCTION

Do you want to write a powerful scene for your novel? Or do you want to troubleshoot a scene that should be a highlight of your story, but somehow falls flat?

This book teaches you professional techniques for making your scenes sparkle.

The first eight chapters show you some approaches you can use for every type of scene, character and location, as well as how to use plot events to structure your scene, how to start and end it, and how to troubleshoot a scene draft that doesn't work.

Then I offer you 20 chapters, each dealing with a specific kind of scene, such as the first and final part of a novel, the black moment and the Climax, creepy scenes, love scenes, erotic scenes, scenes set indoors, outdoors or at night, scenes featuring battles, duels, arguments, confessions, travel, captivity, chases, relationship break-ups and more.

When you're ready to start working on a scene, simply look up the relevant chapters, study the techniques, and decide how to apply them. You may find useful advice in more than one section. For example, the scene you're working on may be at the same time a climax scene, outdoor scene, night scene and duel scene, so there are four chapters offering you advice and inspiration.

This book contains suggestions, not rules. I believe that authors should make their own artistic choices about which techniques to apply and how. There are no formulas that work for every story, and no 'rules' every writer must obey.

Please note that this book is not intended for beginners. I assume that you have mastered the basics of the craft and moved beyond them, so I won't explain what a scene is, why a story needs conflict or how characterisation works. Instead, I focus on advanced and professional techniques. (If you're a novice, you may still pick up useful hints in this book, but won't get the full benefits an experienced writer does.)

Some of the chapters are based on posts I've written for expert blogs, and some sections overlap with the contents of my other books. For example, the chapter 'Fight Scenes' contains in condensed form the main points from *Writing Fight Scenes*, while the chapter 'Scary Scenes' is a short version of *Writing Scary Scenes*, and the chapters on Indoor/Outdoor/Night scenes repeat elements from *Writing Vivid Settings*.

At the end of each chapter, I give you an assignment — sometimes a single sentence to write for your scene — so you can put what you've learned into practice immediately.

I use British English, so the spelling, grammar and vocabulary may look unfamiliar to American readers. I alternate between 'he' and 'she' although the techniques apply to characters of either gender.

Now, let's get started. Decide which scene you want to work on, and make it great.

Rayne Hall

CHAPTER 1

THE CAST OF CHARACTERS

Who are the players in this scene? Make a list of everyone who is present and involved.

WHO IS THE POINT-OF-VIEW?

To immerse the reader into the scene, write it from the perspective of one character. Let the reader see what that character sees, hear what that character hears, smells, touches, thinks and feels during the experience. This pulls the reader deep into the story.

How to choose the best PoV:

- The PoV is the main character (MC) in this scene

- The PoV is present throughout the scene

- The PoV has something at stake

- The PoV is emotionally involved in the events and the outcome

Perhaps the scene's PoV is the same as that of the preceding scene, or perhaps the PoV remains constant throughout the whole book. That's the easiest to handle.

But if the scene presents a new perspective with a different PoV character, you need to make this clear from the start, so the reader won't be confused. To establish quickly who the PoV is now, use a sensory impression. For example: *The icy December wind stung Mary's cheeks.* Or: *The tempting aromas of fried bacon and melted cheese made John's stomach rumble.*

If possible, keep to that one PoV for the whole scene.

WHAT IF THE MAIN CHARACTER IS NOT THE POV?

Sometimes the Main Character (MC) and the Point-of-View (PoV) are different characters. In this case, the MC is the character who has most at stake and who takes action, while the PoV is the insightful observer. Both should be emotionally involved in the events and outcomes.

HOW MANY CHARACTERS PER SCENE?

Do you have more than three characters? That's not a problem, but you will need to write well so the reader won't get confused. If skilfully written, a scene with four, five or even ten characters can work. But if the reader has to concentrate hard to keep up with who is doing what to whom, how and why, she won't enjoy the story much.

If your scene has many characters, consider if you could leave any of them out. If they don't play a real role, drop them.

Avoid introducing more than two new characters in one scene. This is just a guideline of course, not a rule.

You can have walk-on characters, the so-called 'spear-carriers' who aren't really characters, but props. They're not named, and only superficially described, with a mere hint of personality, and they don't affect the outcome of the scene. For example: *A surly waitress took our orders.* Or: *At the market, gnarled peasant women offered potatoes and turnips in woven baskets.*

You can have several of these 'spear-carriers', but make sure not to draw more attention to them, or the reader will expect them to play an important role in the scene.

WHAT YOU NEED TO KNOW ABOUT EACH CHARACTER

Each character wants to get or achieve something in this situation. What is it?

If every character has a goal, the scene will become much more vibrant. More about this in the next chapter.

Also, think about how each character feels about the others. Maybe Mary thinks that John is a tedious know-it-all, while John thinks Mary is a cute but uneducated girl, and Ben admires John uncritically.

Once you're aware of these attitudes, you can hint at them in your scene, and the scene will feel more real.

NOVICE WRITER MISTAKES TO AVOID

Don't use more characters in the scene than are needed. Your scene will be tighter and clearer if you keep the cast small.

Avoid changing the Point-of-View in mid-scene. If at all possible, stick to one PoV per scene, and switch when the next scene starts.

FURTHER STUDIES

To delve deeper into this subject, you may want to progress to my books *Writing Vivid Characters* or *Writing Deep Point Of View*.

ASSIGNMENTS

1. Make a list of the characters you plan to use in this scene. Assess critically if they are needed. If you have more than three, consider eliminating any who don't contribute to the plot.

2. Decide who the scene's PoV character is.

CHAPTER 2

GOALS

Every character in this scene should have a goal, something she wants to achieve in this situation.

Although people in real life sometimes just hang around without a goal, this would be boring in fiction. Give each character a goal, and watch the tension mount.

THE POV'S GOAL

The scene hinges on the main character's goal. What does she want or need?

This goal needs to be very clear — to you, to the character herself, and to the reader. So, state it at the beginning of the scene. Spell it out. Don't just imply it and hope that the reader will get the subtle hints.

Throughout the scene, remind the reader of the MC's goal several times — in the narrative, in dialogue, in thought, or in whatever way is appropriate. Keep it in the reader's mind.

Let's say Mary is the main character (as well as the PoV) of this scene. She needs a boat for the weekend. Her scene goal is to persuade John to lend her his dinghy.

At the beginning of the scene, when Mary rings John's doorbell, you can write: *How could she persuade John to lend her his dinghy for the weekend?*

Perhaps while waiting for John to come home, Mary chats with his sister. *"I need to borrow John's dinghy,"* Mary confessed. *"Do you think he'll lend it to me?"*

When John refuses, write: *She really needed that dinghy. What could she do to make John change his mind?*

Throughout the scene, the character tries to achieve that goal. Perhaps John changes the subject repeatedly, but Mary will always get back to the topic of the boat. She will coax, argue, plead, offer to pay, suggest other favours, promise to take good care of the dinghy, and do whatever she can to get it.

At the end of the scene, it needs to be clear whether the character has achieved her scene goal or not. Perhaps she has achieved it in part, or perhaps she is even further away from it than before.

OTHER CHARACTER'S GOALS

Each character should have a goal. The major characters' goals may be in conflict with the main character's.

Let's say Mary wants to borrow John's dinghy for the weekend. But John's girlfriend Sue wants to borrow it too. Now Mary's and Sue's goals are in conflict.

Or perhaps John wants to paint the dinghy this weekend. He has bought the paint and taken time off work to do this. Now Mary's and John's goals are in conflict.

If John's sister is present when Mary comes to ask for the dinghy, she will have an agenda. What if she's a matchmaker at heart who wants to bring about a romance between Mary and John? Or perhaps her goal is to recruit members for a literature club, or to persuade John to give up smoking. Whatever her goal, it will show in the scene, and it will make the scene more vivid.

Minor characters have goals too. They may be something as simple as 'get out of this meeting before 3 pm' or 'show them that I'm an efficient assistant'. Perhaps John's toddler son wants a chocolate cookie from the tray on the table.

PROFESSIONAL TIP

Perhaps a character wants to keep her goal a secret from some or all of the others. This adds tension and suspense.

Give some thought as to whether the other characters are aware of the MC's goal and how they feel about it. Does John's sister know that Mary wants to borrow the dinghy? Does his girlfriend?

Mary may tell them openly what she wants. But perhaps she doesn't want John's sister and girlfriend to know of her plans, and this can add spice to the scene.

If you want to be devious, arrange it so that even John doesn't know what Mary is really after! Perhaps she pretends that she's dropped in to get his famous chocolate cookie recipe. Or maybe she earnestly asks his advice on buying her own dinghy... while secretly manipulating the situation so he will offer her the loan of his boat of his own accord. In this she may or may not succeed.

NOVICE WRITER MISTAKES TO AVOID

Don't be vague about the goal, or rely on hints.

ASSIGNMENT

What is the main character's goal? What will she do to achieve it?

Find three or more ways to reiterate the goal in the scene.

CHAPTER 3

CONFLICTS

Give your scene two conflicts: an outer conflict and an inner conflict. If possible, relate both to the MC's scene goal.

Here's how to do it.

OUTER CONFLICT

The MC's goal clashes with that of one (or several) of the other characters.

Let's say Mary's goal is to persuade John to lend her his dinghy for the weekend. But John refuses, because his goal is to take the lovely Sue on a sailing trip on Sunday.

Or perhaps Mary's goal in this scene is to escape from the serial killer's clutches. The serial killer, on the other hand, has the goal to dismember and kill his captive.

Both try their utmost, but only one of them can win.

INNER CONFLICT

The MC's goal clashes with a deeply-held inner value. She can achieve what she wants — but only if she goes against her conscience or beliefs.

If you've developed Mary as a fully fleshed-out character, you'll know what her main values are. Which of them might prove an obstacle to attaining her goal?

Let's say Mary is a truthful person who values honesty above almost everything else. She could persuade John to lend her the dinghy if she lied about her reasons for needing it. Assuming that she really needs the boat (perhaps to catch the serial killer or to rescue her children), this creates a terrible dilemma. Should she, or shouldn't she, tell a lie?

Or maybe chastity is an important value for Mary. She would never act seductively, especially not towards a married man like John. But she knows that John is a bit of a lecher who has the hots for her. If she were to open the top buttons of her blouse and hint at sexual favours she might grant, he'd be sure to soften and let her borrow the boat. And she really, really needs that boat. What will she do?

NOVICE WRITER MISTAKES TO AVOID

Don't write a scene without a conflict. Ideally, your scene should have both inner and outer conflicts.

PROFESSIONAL TIP

Modulate the conflicts. To relax and build tension in the scene, let the conflicts subside and escalate.

Let's say Mary has as almost persuaded John to lend her the dinghy. At this stage, the conflict subsides and tension relaxes.

But then John discovers that Mary has lied to him. He can't trust her, so now he is adamant that he won't lend her the boat. Moreover, he will also warn his neighbours not to lend their boats to Mary, either. Now the conflict escalates, and the tension rises.

FURTHER STUDY

If you want to delve deeper into the 'inner conflict' topic, my book *Writing Vivid Characters* will offer useful insights.

ASSIGNMENT

Identify the main outer conflict, and the main inner conflict, in your scene. Think of ways to intensify them.

CHAPTER 4

LOCATION AND WEATHER

To make your scene vibrant and 'real', be specific about the location. This may mean a real place, but it can also mean a specific type of location: the characters dine not simply in a restaurant, but an upmarket gourmet restaurant in London's West End, an authentic Chinese restaurant famous for its duck dishes in Stockholm, or a rustic pizzeria in Naples. Instead of walking in a generic forest, let them ramble up the steep slopes of a pine wood in Turkey, beneath the gold-speckled autumn canopy of a beech wood in southern Germany, or in a fir forest in Yellowstone National Park.

Be equally clear about the season, the time of the day and the weather. To perceive the story as real, the reader needs to know that it's an early afternoon in late spring. Whether it's 5.15pm on the 28th of March or 5.20pm on the 19th doesn't matter for most types of stories. But a broad idea is crucial.

Be specific because this will make the scene feel 'real' to the reader.

The season, time of the day and weather give the scene a specific atmosphere and make the characters act in specific ways.

Let's say John holds a barbecue party in his garden.

Is it Sunday lunchtime after church, on a mild, sun-bright day at the end of May? Or, is it going on midnight on the 31st of December, surrounded by darkness and snow? Perhaps it's a damp autumn day, and the fire won't light, and then the wind blows acrid smoke into everyone's nostrils. Each of these scenarios can form a great backdrop for your scene... but each will be very different.

NOVICE WRITER MISTAKES TO AVOID

Inexperienced writers often shy away from committing to a specific time, place and weather. They use a generic 'village' or 'garden' which could be anywhere, with nondescript weather and no clue about the season or the time of the day. As a result, their scenes don't come alive.

PROFESSIONAL TIP

If you want to make your scene exciting and emotionally intense, use extreme weather, such as a heatwave, a severe storm or a heavy deluge.

FURTHER STUDY

For more detailed suggestions about using the location and weather in your scene, see the chapters on Indoor Scenes and Outdoor Scenes.

If you're interested in this topic and want to explore it in greater depth, I recommend my book *Writing Vivid Settings*.

ASSIGNMENT

Write a sentence showing either the weather or its effects on a character.

CHAPTER 5

PLOT EVENTS

Plot events are the things that happen in the scene, especially what the MC does. They move the MC either closer to her goal or further away from it.

A plot event always involves action. Thoughts and feelings alone don't constitute an event.

Examples:

Mary feels hurt by John's betrayal. This is not a plot event.

Feeling hurt by John's betrayal, Mary destroys his boat in revenge. This is a plot event.

Mary regrets stealing the dinghy. This is not a plot event.

When the police arrest Mary, she regrets stealing the dinghy. This is a plot event.

How many plot events should your scene have? Between three and five per scene usually works well, but some scenes may have more or fewer.

TYPICAL SCENE STRUCTURE

You may follow this pattern for structuring your scene:

- Beginning

- Plot Event 1

- Plot Event 2

- Plot Event 3

- Plot Event 4

- Ending

NOVICE WRITER MISTAKES TO AVOID

Inexperienced writers often have plot events which are non-events where nothing happens. The MC emotes a lot but doesn't act. The resulting scenes feel static and dragging.

PROFESSIONAL TIP

You can make the MC's emotions the trigger or the consequence of the action.

Examples:

When John breaks his word and betrays her, Mary feels hurt.

Hurt by John's betrayal, Mary takes revenge and destroys his boat.

ASSIGNMENT

Using the 'Typical Scene Structure' pattern, structure your scene. Identify each plot event clearly. You may vary the number of plot events.

CHAPTER 6

HOW TO START THE SCENE

The beginning of your scene — the first 100 words or so — should provide the following information.

All of these:

- who the PoV is
- MC's scene goal
- a clue about the location

As many as possible of these:

- clue about the season
- clue about the time of day
- clue about the weather
- inner conflict
- outer conflict
- MC's state of mind

None of these items need to be particularly detailed. Just a clue is all the reader needs at this stage. You can deliver the details later in the scene.

Of course, you need to present this information in a way that hooks the reader, so she simply must read the scene even though she had meant to put the book down for the day. Herein lies the difficulty. Faced with the need to provide several pieces of information, many writers create 'info-dumps' at the start of their scenes, and those don't hook readers.

Keep the beginning short and vibrant. The trick is to make each sentence serve several purposes.

With a bit of thought, you should be able to convey two or more of the elements from the above list in a single sentence.

Here are some examples. Your own writing style will of course be different, but you can use these for inspiration.

The rain-slick asphalt reflected the flickering colours of the neon advertising signs. These twelve words tell the reader that it's night, that it's raining, and that the scene is set in an urban location.

The snow-laden January wind stung Mary's cheeks. In seven words this sentence shows four elements from the list: that Mary is the PoV, that it's January, that the setting is outdoors, and that the weather is windy and cold.

NOVICE WRITER MISTAKES TO AVOID

Inexperienced writers often draft lengthy scene openings, weighed down with explanations and detailed setting descriptions.

PROFESSIONAL TIP

Smells work well at the beginning of a scene. They can unobtrusively establish the PoV and the location, and sometimes the time of the day or the season, too.

Examples:

The air smelled of barbecues, wood smoke and freshly mown grass.

The scent of hot roasted chestnuts and gingerbread made Mary's stomach growl with hunger.

ASSIGNMENT

Craft one sentence containing three of the clues from the list, to incorporate into your scene beginning. Really use your writing skill to create a sentence that conveys the information without feeling like an 'info dump'.

CHAPTER 7

HOW TO END THE SCENE

The end of the scene needs to fulfill two purposes: to show clearly whether the MC achieved her goal, and to lead the reader to the next scene.

HAS THE MC ACHIEVED HER GOAL?

The answer can be any of these:

- Yes, she has

- No, she hasn't

- Yes, she has, but there's a drawback

- No, she hasn't, but she's achieved something else

- No, she hasn't, and furthermore, things are worse for her than before

The last three — 'yes but', 'no but', 'no and furthermore' — are more nuanced and therefore more interesting than a bland 'yes' or 'no'.

LEADING INTO THE NEXT SCENE

A smooth way to lead into the next scene is to have the MC (who is also the PoV) evaluate the events, and decide on her next action.

Kneading her quadriceps to ease the stiffness in her legs, Mary replayed the day's competitions in her mind over and over. She had lost three matches out of four — her worst ever performance. She would have to do better next week.

Was Sue the superior athlete she appeared to be — or did she have a hidden advantage? Mary had six days to improve her own performance and discover Sue's secret.

THE SO-CALLED 'SEQUEL'

The word 'sequel' in the context of writing has several meanings. One of them is the part of the scene when the ending is over, and the MC reflects on what happened.

Some writers use a structuring method called 'Scene & Sequel' in which action (called 'scene') alternates with reflection (called 'sequel'). In this approach, all the plot events are part of the 'scene', while the ending is the 'sequel'.

Be careful to get the balance right. Inexperienced writers give equal weight to 'scene' and 'sequel' (i.e. to action and reflection). The result is a story in which the characters think, ponder, consider, muse and feel a lot, evaluate events and analyse their feelings. Mary, having lost a sports competition, thinks about her performance, her opponent, the referees, her training, and her unhappy childhood, feels disappointed, frustrated, hopeless, considers herself a failure and so on. This can read more like a psychotherapy session than an exciting novel.

To avoid this trap, keep the 'sequel' part short, and make it dynamic. The character reflects on what happened, what went wrong, mistakes she's made... and then plans how to improve her performance and what step to take next.

CREATING CLIFFHANGERS

You can break off a scene at an exciting moment, when the main character is in a dire situation of great danger, metaphorically dangling from a cliff. The reader simply must know if (or how) the MC will get out of this, so instead of putting the book down as she had planned, she turns to the next page.

Careful: if you simply break off the scene and start a new one where you left off, the story may lose its natural 'flow'.

Try to break off at a moment where the MC can't take any action and is compelled to wait — for example, while she is tied up in the serial killer's dungeon, unable to move.

Then switch to another location and another PoV character for the next scene.

The scene after that returns to the original MC and location, showing her escape from the dungeon or fight the serial killer.

This approach can create enormous suspense.

NOVICE WRITER MISTAKES TO AVOID

Don't end with the MC reflecting on what has happened without resolving further action and planning the next step.

PROFESSIONAL TIP

Vary the types of scene endings. Mix up scenes ending with 'yes but', 'no but' and 'no and furthermore'. Use cliffhangers sparingly, perhaps only in the most thrilling sections of your novel.

FURTHER STUDY

To learn in-depth novel plotting skills, you may want to study my book *Writing Vivid Plots*.

ASSIGNMENT

Decide whether or not your MC has achieved her scene goal (and whether there's a 'but' or a 'furthermore' attached).

If the MC is also the PoV, write a few sentences in which she mentally reviews what has happened, and plans her next step.

CHAPTER 8

TROUBLE-SHOOTING A WEAK SCENE

You've written a scene, but on paper the draft doesn't come to life the way you envisaged it in your mind. Or perhaps you liked it, but your critique partners and beta readers told you it doesn't work.

Here are some common 'flaws' and how to fix them.

MY SCENE IS TOO LONG

When a scene sprawls over far more pages than any of the other scenes in the book, you have several options.

1. Split it into two scenes. Perhaps there's a natural break somewhere? If yes, move the characters to a new location — perhaps from the living room into the garden, or from the restaurant to the pub — to give each scene a different feel. Change the cast a little, so that one of the characters is not present in both parts.

2. Reduce the cast of characters. The fewer characters, the shorter the scene. Could you eliminate a character or two? Perhaps one character can take on the function of several.

3. Condense the time frame. Over what period does the scene play out? If your draft allows the events to unfold over two hours, condense this to twenty minutes. Think about how the scene would play out in that reduced time, and rewrite it accordingly.

MY SCENE IS TOO SHORT

Put another serious obstacle in the way of the MC achieving her scene goal, and force her to deal with this problem on the spot. This will add another plot event to the scene.

Is the scene still too short? Add another. But stay focused on the MC's goal.

MY SCENE IS BLAND

1. If your scene fails to stir the reader, infuse it with passion — the MC's passion for her goal. What are her reasons for needing to achieve this goal? Make the reasons more important. Make sure she has a lot at stake. Give her the urgent passion to succeed.

2. Add extreme weather — a blizzard, a hurricane, a heatwave, a hailstorm. This little trick can make a big difference.

MY SCENE DRAGS

1. Focus more tightly on the MC's scene goal, the obstacles she encounters and the actions she takes to achieve what she wants. Tighten or cut anything that's not related to the MC's goal.

2. Cut lengthy descriptions of scenery, interiors, characters, anything. Readers skip lengthy descriptions, so keep your descriptions brief but vivid.

3. Analyse your dialogue. Are your characters using more words than they need to get their points across? Do they repeat themselves? Tighten the dialogue to make it razor-sharp.

MY SCENE IS BORING.

If your critique partners tell you that a scene is boring because not enough happens, kick your main character's backside to propel her into action.

1. What's her goal for the scene? What are the obstacles? Tweak the obstacles so she must take more vigorous action to overcome them.

   Try to arrange it so that at least some of the action is physical, not just talking. Perhaps Mary needs to run to catch a bus, squeeze under a bed to hide from the serial killer, row the dingy to the island, pull up the carpet to search for the hidden clue.

2. Give your MC a time limit within which she must attain her goal, and drastic consequences if she fails to do this on time. Perhaps Mary must escape from the dungeon before the clock strikes two, otherwise she will be blown up by the bomb the villain has planted in the house. Maybe she must reach the island before the leaking dinghy sinks. Or, maybe she must return to her coffin before daylight touches her delicate vampire skin.

3. If not much happens in this scene, consider scrapping it. Do you really need the scene? Perhaps it could be summed up in a few words at the beginning of the next real scene. Let's say the boring scene consists of Mary cleaning the house. If you scrap it, you can instead start the next scene with *After four hours of scrubbing and scouring, Mary...*

4. Another solution is to combine the scene with another, letting the events play out simultaneously. Perhaps the problem scene features two characters declaring their love for each other over dinner in a fine restaurant. This important moment in the couple's relationship should stir the reader's emotions... but somehow, it falls flat. What if you combine it with one of the other scenes, perhaps the one where they're hiding from the serial killer, or the one where they work to rescue earthquake victims?

MY SCENE IS CONFUSING

Add clarity by stripping distracting elements. Focus on the MC and her main goal. Cut sub-plots and drop extraneous characters.

Reiterate the MC's goal several times during the scene. This helps the reader focus on what's essential. Whenever an obstacle arises and the MC takes action to deal with it, emphasise that she's doing this in order to attain her goal.

HOW LONG SHOULD A SCENE BE?

There's no rule about the 'right' length of scenes. Mine tend to be 700-1500 words long, but yours may be longer or shorter.

In a novel, the early scenes tend to be the longest. As the pacing speeds up and the excitement increases, the scenes may get shorter — until the Climax which is often the longest scene in the whole book.

Try to keep the scene length reasonably consistent, so the longest scene has no more than three times the word count of the shortest one. However, this is just a guideline, not a firm rule.

NOVICE WRITER MISTAKES TO AVOID

Inexperienced writers often assume that a scene is exciting because it felt exciting when they imagined it in their heads. They don't realise that on paper, it's confusing or dull.

PROFESSIONAL TIP

Swap critiques with other writers, especially writers in your own genre. The more critiques you receive, the better. You don't need to take every piece of advice you receive, because different readers have different tastes. However, if several critiquers say that a certain scene is confusing (or boring, or bland) take note and remedy the problem.

ASSIGNMENT

1. If you have a complete draft manuscript, consider which scenes are the most important. Are they as powerful and exciting as your story deserves? If not, consider what's wrong.

2. Find critique partners either for your complete manuscript draft or for an individual scene. Gather as many critiques as you can get. Now, look for a recurring theme in the feedback. Have several critiquers pointed out the same weakness in a scene?

CHAPTER 9

NOVEL-OPENING SCENES

Do you have an idea for a novel and wonder where to start, or is the first scene of your completed draft not as grabbing as the story deserves?

Here are some pointers. Like everything in this guide, they are suggestions, not rules, and it's up to you to choose what works best for your book.

START CLOSE TO THE ACTION

Inviting readers to your story is like having guests for dinner. Once they've arrived, don't keep them waiting. The pie should already be baking in the oven, filling the room with enticing smells. You may welcome your guests with a drink and small talk, but then it's time to serve the meal. Don't go to the kitchen to start cooking now.

From the first page, readers need to sense that something exciting is about to happen. Don't keep them waiting for long.

HOOK THE READERS

Place at least one 'hook' in the first five sentences, something to grab your readers' interest so they simply have to read on. Different hooks work for different readers. Choose hooks which entice readers of your genre. The mere mention of a bachelor with a rakish reputation may get Regency Romance readers excited, but it won't arouse fans of Police Procedural Thrillers.

STATE THE STORY GOAL

The main character wants something. What is it? State it as early and clearly as possible. Readers root for characters who have a goal. The principle is the same as with a scene goal (explained in Chapter 2), only it relates to the whole novel. What does the MC want or need to achieve in the book?

This is likely to be a big goal — save a wildlife preserve, catch the serial killer, find true love. The scene goals of the various scenes in the book are often steps the MC needs to take to achieve the story goal.

Thus, the novel's first scene often shows two goals: the story goal (what the MC needs to achieve in the end) and the scene goal (what she needs to achieve in this scene). State the scene goal during the first few sentences, and the story goal when the MC forms it.

This can create an interesting situation: The MC thinks she needs to solve a certain problem (scene goal), but then discovers that she actually has a much bigger problem to solve (story goal).

FOUR TYPES OF BEGINNINGS

1. **Dialogue**

    When you start the novel with dialogue, the story feels vivid from the start. This is also a great way to introduce characters and conflicts.

    Stick to two characters, because more speakers would confuse the reader who hasn't met these people before. Make it clear who is saying what. Avoid info-dumping dialogue where speakers explain to one another things they already know.

2. **Setting**

    Opening with the setting allows you to set the mood for the scene and the whole book — tense, creepy, humorous. It also conveys the scene's location, the season and the time of the day, as well as the Point-of-View character's state of mind.

    Avoid lengthy setting descriptions without character or action. Put the character into the setting, let him or her move in or interact with it. If you're writing deep Point-of-View, show the setting from the PoV character's perspective. Use several senses — not just vision, but sound and smell, and perhaps touch and temperature.

3. **Action**

This opening is exciting, and it promises the readers that they're in for a thrilling ride. The characters chase a fugitive, hoist a sail, rehearse a show, escape from prison, build a wall, wrestle a villain, forge a sword or do something else relevant to the plot.

To tap into this excitement, the readers need to know why the character is fighting, working, chasing, fleeing, otherwise they have no emotional investment. If several characters are involved, focus on just two of them, otherwise the readers get confused.

4. **Exposition**

Telling the reader who the characters are, explaining their background and current situation, and giving an overview of the social conditions was an acceptable way to start a novel in the 19th century. Authors could devote several pages to explanations before allowing the story to take off.

Most modern readers don't have the patience for this. They want to read a story, not explanations. Unless you're consciously imitating 19th century style — perhaps for a parody — I suggest you avoid this approach.

NINE OVER-USED NOVEL STARTS

Most novels by novice authors start with one of the same nine beginnings.

Although these starts are not wrong, they are unlikely to get your novel selected for publication. Put yourself in the mind of an agent or editor reading submissions. If she's seen the same opening twelve times already that day, yours won't grab her interest.

It's OK if your draft begins with one of these openings, because they're a useful exercise for the writer to transition into the story, but you may want to change it before you submit the manuscript for publication.

1. **Getting out of Bed**

   The character wakes in the morning, gets up, brushes his teeth, dresses and packs while thinking about the day ahead.

2. **The Disoriented Wake-up**

   The character wakes up wondering where he is and how he got there.

3. **The Journey**

   The character walks (or drives, rides, sails, flies) to the destination. On the way he reflects on his life history and on the social conditions and politics of the place.

4. **The Captain Hears Alarm**

   The captain/sergeant/team leader of a police/military/paramilitary/medical/other unit is engaging in a peaceful activity (typically having a drink with his comrades) when suddenly the alarm bell rings/the siren howls/the red light flashes. In the resulting scramble, he rallies his team to deal with the emergency.

5. **The Wardrobe**

   Standing in front of her wardrobe, the character considers what to wear for an upcoming event.

6. **The Mirror**

   The character sits in front of the mirror, beautifying herself for the event and contemplating her looks.

7. **Waiting in a Bar**

The character sits in a bar (sometimes in a coffee shop, restaurant, hotel lobby or pub) waiting for someone (usually a stranger) whom he is supposed to meet here. The person is late.

8. **The Writer Writes**

The novelist sits at her computer, thinking about a story she is going to write.

9. **The Window Gaze**

The character gazes out of the window, reflecting upon his present, past and future.

PROFESSIONAL TIP

Be devious. Begin with the MC pursuing the scene goal. Then make her realise that she has a much bigger problem... and that the pursuit of the scene goal has made that big problem worse! To achieve the story goal, she needs to undo the scene goal she's accomplished.

This twist doesn't work for every novel, but if it fits the plot, it presents an opening that grabs readers in a big way.

NOVICE WRITER MISTAKES TO AVOID

Besides starting too far away from the action or using over-used beginnings, many novice writers make one of these mistakes which put readers off:

1. **Four-Letter Words**

In a desperate bid for attention, many new writers start with a swearword: "Damn!" "Hell!" "Fuck!" This method worked to shock readers (and editors) to attention 100 years ago. Today's readers are just bored.

2. **Confusing the Reader**

   Trying to intrigue the reader, new writers often write nebulous openings. But instead of growing curious, the reader who doesn't understand what's going on simply puts the book or manuscript down and reads something else.

3. **Haha — I Got You**

   Another desperate ploy to get attention is the fake opening. The author presents the character in an exciting situation — and at the end of the scene, this is revealed to have been merely a dream/a computer game/a simulation exercise.

4. **Flashbacks**

   Many inexperienced writers flash back to what happened before the story's beginning, on the first page. This is not a good idea, because the reader doesn't yet care about the characters' past. Postpone major flashbacks until later scenes when the reader has become interested in this person. If a flashback is necessary in the first scene, keep it as short as possible.

ASSIGNMENT

1. If you have a complete draft, check the first scene against the above lists of overused novel openings and novice mistakes. Does it have one of these weaknesses? If yes, consider writing a different opening scene.

2. If you're starting a new novel — or if you've decided to rewrite the opening scene of your draft — decide which of the four types of openings would suit the story best.

CHAPTER 10

BLACK MOMENT SCENES

Most novels have a Black Moment when all seems lost before the main character resolves to try again and rallies all her strength for the big confrontation at the novel's climax.

The Black Moment adds drama, excitement and emotional depth to the novel's middle part. If your draft suffers from a sagging middle, adding or improving a Black Moment can be the solution. Here are professional techniques you can use:

- Place the Black Moment in the middle of your novel or a little later. Two thirds into the book often works well.

- Internal and external conflicts increase to a level where the MC can't bear it anymore.

- Arrange it so everything and everyone has turned against the main character at this stage. Make it as difficult as you possibly can: His girlfriend has broken up with him, his allies have deserted the cause, he has been fired from his job and evicted from his home, the villain's henchmen are closing in, and his big secret has been exposed in the press. To make matters worse, his daughter has been abducted and will die unless the hero surrenders the proof of the villain's machinations... and he can neither rescue her nor deliver the documents because he's locked up in a prison cell. Really pile it on.

- Make it still more difficult by taking away his means of communication — the mobile phone (British) or cell phone (American), the internet connection, the humans who might carry a message.

- Turn the suspense volume up as high as you can. The 'ticking clock' technique works well. The hero has only a certain amount of time — perhaps one hour — to escape from the villain's clutches and rescue his girlfriend, defuse the bomb or save the world. He is aware of the time ticking away. You can emphasise this by actually showing a clock. The hero sees he has thirty minutes left... then fifteen... ten...five...two...one. This builds enormous suspense.

- The Black Moment doesn't have to be about high action, but can be a situation of quiet desperation. In the Romance genre, it may simply be that the heroine has lost her lover and there seems no chance of winning him back.

- All seems lost. Only a tiny shred of hope remains that the MC will achieve her big, important goal.

- The MC feels disappointed, disheartened, betrayed, desperate, helpless.

- If the plot allows, consider adding fear to this cocktail of emotions. He fears not only for himself, but for the safety of his abducted girlfriend, as well as for the people in the building the villain is about to bomb, for the survival of the human race, or whatever is at stake in your story.

- Let the reader feel the hero's physical responses to the tension: the aching neck, the dry throat, the sweat trickling down his sides.

- During this Black Moment, the main character may also learn unwelcome truths about herself. In many novels, this is when immense character growth happens.

- At the end of the Black Moment', either as part of the same scene or in a separate scene, something happens that convinces her that she must make one more attempt. She rallies her last ounce of strength and courage, re-commits to the cause, and gets ready to try once more. (This final attempt, in which she risks everything, will be the book's climax. In the next chapter, we'll look at how to write the Climax scene.)

- If you've structured your novel with the 'Hero's Journey' plot model (after Joseph Campbell's theory), the Black Moment equals the so-called 'Ordeal' section.

The more desperate you make the 'Black Moment,' the more exciting the Climax and the more rewarding the End.

NOVICE MISTAKES TO AVOID

Inexperienced writers are too kind to their characters, making the Black Moment not devastating enough, or don't flesh it out into a full scene.

PROFESSIONAL TIP

The Black Moment is a descent into darkness — physical, emotional, mental, psychological or spiritual, or even all of those.

To increase the metaphorical 'descent into darkness', consider locating the scene literally underground. The effect will be amazing. How about a storage cellar, a castle dungeon, an abandoned mine shaft, a nuclear fallout bunker, a cave?

FURTHER STUDIES

If you want to learn skills for plotting the overall novel, including how to work with the 'Hero's Journey' model, I suggest *Writing Vivid Plots*.

ASSIGNMENT

Take the scene you have drafted or planned for the novel's 'Black Moment'. How can you make the situation still worse for the MC? Pile it on.

CHAPTER 11

CLIMAX SCENES

The main character has just overcome the trials of the Black Moment and the plot races to its conclusion. Now the MC has to face the greatest challenge — perhaps a confrontation with the antagonist — and the tension is so high that the reader perches on the edge of her seat, unable to tear herself away from the story's action.

This is the big scene the reader has been waiting for, so make sure it meets her expectations — or better still, exceeds them.

Study the Climax scenes of bestselling novels in your genre, and use them as inspiration for the structure, content and style of yours.

Here are some tips on how to power up your climax scene to keep your reader enthralled.

1. Give it time and space. Don't rush the Climax scene or skip over details. Develop it as a full scene, perhaps the longest scene in the book.

2. Choose an unusual location, preferably one which is weird or dangerous — or both. How about a steep rock face in the mountains, a rope bridge across a ravine, the rooftop of a skyscraper, a derelict amusement park, a raft racing towards a cataract?

3. What lessons has the MC learnt? During the course of the novel, he has grown, overcome bad habits, gained control over his weakness and reconsidered his values. The Climax tests this. Has he truly left his old self behind, will he act according to his recently acquired insight, and will his new values stand firm in the face of the challenge?

4. During the Climax scene, the MC should come across as honourable, resourceful and brave.

5. Arrange it so the protagonist (main character) and the antagonist (opponent, villain) face each other in a final showdown. If your first draft doesn't have a protagonist/antagonist showdown at the Climax, consider changing the plot to bring one about; readers will love you for it.

6. Emphasise how much is at stake — the MC's survival, her marriage, her happiness, the life of a child, the safety of her nation, the rescue of an endangered species or world peace. More than one thing can be at stake.

7. Stack the odds against the main character — for example, the opponent is better prepared, and has superior equipment while the MC is unarmed, exhausted, unprepared, perhaps even injured.

8. Throw some surprises into the plot: the arrival of a character who shouldn't be there, support from an unlikely source, and unexpected obstacles which make the challenge for the MC even tougher.

9. Does the MC have a special skill? Perhaps he's a trained acrobat, a champion jockey, an inscrutable poker player or an ace violinist? Is he good at charming people, or can he remember numbers like no one else? Whatever his special skill, let him use it in the Climax scene.

10. Aim to arouse intense emotions in the reader — not just one feeling, but several. The mix of emotions depends on the genre and your individual story. For example, terror is a perfect emotion for the Climax of a Horror novel, but it would not be desirable in a Romance. Excitement is always a good choice when combined with others. Think about the emotions you want your readers to feel during this scene, and then set about arousing them.

11. Make the Climax scene as exciting as you can, perhaps even scary. How scary depends on the genre. In a Thriller or Horror

novel, scare your readers to the utmost. But even in a Romance, Chicklit novel or Comedy, it's worth adding an element of danger to increase the excitement. Perhaps the characters meet in a terrifying location or engage in a perilous activity. If your MC has a phobia, force her to face her fear during the Climax. If she has a phobia of heights, make her scale a cliff to rescue the child. If she's terrified of being underground, locate the Climax scene in a deep cave. The reader will feel her fear.

NOVICE WRITER MISTAKES TO AVOID

Inexperienced authors often write short, rushed, 'skimpy' Climax scenes, not realising that this is the most important scene of the book, the one by which the reader will judge and remember the reading experience.

PROFESSIONAL TIP

To add emotional depth and tension, include a moment of self-doubt when the MC wonders if she is doing the right thing or if she has the courage to follow through on her decision. She may even waver in her resolution and be tempted to return to her old ways. However, keep this moment short, perhaps just a couple of sentences. The MC's prevailing attitude in this scene should be courage and confidence.

FURTHER STUDIES

If you want to study novel plotting, consider *Writing Vivid Plots*.

ASSIGNMENT

Think of ways to make the Climax scene in your novel as exciting as possible. (Can you stake the odds against the MC? What's the most dangerous location where this scene could play out? What unexpected event could increase the thrill?)

CHAPTER 12

WRITING NOVEL-CLOSING SCENES

The final scene shapes the readers' lasting impression of the novel. If they love the ending, they'll remember the story, tell their friends about it, and look for more works by the same author.

How can you create the powerful ending your novel deserves?

SATISFY THE READER

The ending must satisfy the readers. They have spent many hours in the company of the characters, have suffered with them and cheered them on, and now they need to know that it was worthwhile.

Don't disappoint your readers — they would not forgive you if you let them down now. Reward them for their patience and loyalty, and create an ending that satisfies.

A 'satisfying' ending doesn't necessarily mean a happy one, although this depends on the genre and the readers' expectations.

To satisfy, the ending must above all answer the question posed at the novel's beginning. In your opening scene, you planted a question in the reader's mind: "Will this person achieve this goal?" (Or a variation of this, e.g. "How will this person achieve this goal?") You may want to re-read the chapter 'Goals'.

The novel's final scene needs to provide a definite answer — and the answer doesn't always have to be "yes".

TYPES OF ENDINGS

Happy Ending: "Yes."

The main character has achieved her goal: *Yes, she has saved the butterfly habitat. Yes, she got that man. Yes, she has rescued the hostages.*

A plain 'yes' ending works for many types of novel, but it may feel shallow and is unlikely to leave a lasting impression.

Extremely Happy Ending: "Yes, and moreover..."

The main character has achieved her goal, and on top of that, she has gained something wonderful and unexpected:

Yes, she has saved the butterfly habitat, and her campaign has led to a change in legislation, protecting all her country's wildlife habitats.

Yes, she got that man, and she has also gained recognition for her performing art.

Yes, she has rescued the hostages, and she has also found love with Special Agent John.

This type of ending works well for Romance and for fiction of an upbeat nature.

Happily Ever After: "Yes, and it will last."

The main character has achieved her goal, and it's obvious that the wonderful thing is going to last.

Yes, she has saved the butterfly habitat, and on top of that she has received the funding to secure its future.

Yes, she got that man, and it's clear that together they will be able to deal with any challenges the future may throw at them.

Yes, she has rescued the hostages, and the terrorists won't be able to take hostages ever again.

This type of ending is popular in Romance fiction (often in combination with 'Extremely Happy Ending'). It is deeply satisfying, because the reader feels the solution isn't a shallow short-term fix. It works best for novels with a strong character arc.

Moderately Happy Ending: "Yes, but…"

The main character has achieved her goal, but at a price. She has lost or sacrificed something to attain this goal:

Yes, she has saved the butterfly habitat, but her boyfriend has dumped her.

Yes, she got that man, but only by sacrificing the chance to star in a musical.

Yes, she has saved the hostages, but her colleague Special Agent John got killed in the process.

This approach works for most genres. You can vary the degree of happiness by making the sacrifice either small or significant. If the loss was terrible (the death of wonderful Special Agent John), then you can have your readers in tears at the end of the book (but feel deeply satisfied). If the loss is minor (e.g. she had to give up one theatre role, but can resume her performing career with another), then you have effectively a happy ending, but one that feels realistic and avoids being cheesy.

Unhappy Ending: "No."

The main character hasn't achieved her goal.

No, she hasn't managed to save the butterfly habitat.

No, she didn't get that man.

No, she didn't save the hostages.

This type of ending is frustrating as well as shallow. Readers seldom find this satisfactory.

Extremely Unhappy Ending: "No, and moreover..."

The main character hasn't achieved her goal, and on top of that, something seriously bad happens to her.

No, she didn't save the butterfly habitat, and moreover the love of her life married someone else.

No, she didn't get that man, and moreover she had both legs amputated.

No, she didn't rescue the hostages, and moreover Special Agent John got killed because of her mistake.

This type of ending sometimes works for a short story, but rarely for a novel. Readers who've spent hours rooting for this character would find it deeply disappointing.

Moderately Unhappy Ending: "No, but..."

The main character hasn't achieved her goal, but she has gained something else.

No, she didn't save the butterfly habitat, but she found like-minded people.

No, she didn't get that man, but she got engaged to a better one.

No, she didn't rescue the hostages, but she found love with Special Agent John.

If the unexpected gain is small, it provides a solace to the reader, so that the ending is unhappy, but not without hope. If the unexpected gain is greater than the goal she strove for, the result is a muted, but believable, hopeful happiness which works well for the Historical and Religious/Inspirational genres. This type of ending often has a bitter-sweet flavour.

Open Ending: "Second thoughts."

The character is in the position to achieve the goal, but has second thoughts. With what she learned over the course of the story, she is no longer sure that she wants it:

She can save the butterfly habitat... but realises that by doing so she would permanently destroy an endangered dragonfly species.

That man proposes marriage, but she is no longer sure he's the one she wants.

She can free the hostages... but she knows that they are dangerous terrorists, not innocent victims as she had believed.

To make an open ending satisfactory, the reader needs to know that the main character now has the power to decide the outcome. Only the question, 'what will she do?' remains, and if you handle it well, this question will haunt the reader for a long time.

STIR EMOTIONS

For your novel's ending, really tug at the reader's heartstrings. Make them smile or cry, clench or warm their hearts, in a way that suits the story and the genre. The more emotional you can make the ending, the stronger the impression the reader takes away from the book. Then the story will stay in their mind for a long time, and they'll discuss the book with other readers, and eagerly look for more novels by the same author.

CONCLUDE THE CHARACTER ARC

The main character needs to have grown during the story. She has become a wiser person, and probably a better one. What lesson has she learned? In what way has she changed for the better?

In the closing scene, you need to prove that she has really changed. Insert the kind of incident that used to trigger her character flaw... and she behaves differently.

LEAVING THREADS UNTIED

If the novel is part of a series, or if you plan to write a sequel, it's a good idea to leave at least one thread untied, to pick up in the next volume. A question that remains unanswered can become part of the next book's plot.

However, this should be a question related to a subplot, not the main story question, or the readers will not feel satisfied.

For example, in a thriller, the main plot (rescue of the hostages) is resolved. But the subplot — the sizzling undercurrents in her relationship with Special Agent John — is unresolved. Will they, or won't they, become a couple? You can keep the 'Will they, or won't they become a couple?' question unanswered over several books, until the conclusion of the series. Each book has a separate main plot, and that gets resolved by the end of the book.

CLIFFHANGERS

A 'Cliffhanger' is an ending that occurs just before something exciting is about to happen. Cliffhangers are normally used at the end of a chapter or scene to keep readers turning the page. (You may want to re-read the chapter 'How To End The Scene').

Some authors apply the same principle to the end of a book, so that readers buy the next volume in the series to find out what happens.

However, most readers find Cliffhanger' endings unsatisfactory. They've read the book to get the answer to the story question, only to find that this answer has been withheld.

The Cliffhanger' marketing strategy can work if the sequel is immediately available. But if the next book in your series won't be published for a year, or if you haven't even written it yet, you'll have a lot of frustrated readers instead of loyal fans.

NOVICE WRITER MISTAKES TO AVOID

Inexperienced writers sometimes create an open ending that doesn't answer the story questions. After reading the book, readers still haven't found out whether or not the main character can achieve her goal. Don't make this mistake. It will leave your readers frustrated, and you will have missed the chance to create an ending that satisfies.

Another beginner mistake is to finish the novel with the Climax. This makes the ending feel rushed, and doesn't give the readers the payoff they've been waiting for. The Climax deserves a scene of its own, probably the one before the ending. (Re-read the chapter 'Climax Scenes'.)

PROFESSIONAL TIP

Even if you intend the novel as a stand-alone and have no plans for a series, keep your options open by leaving some minor threads untied. If the book becomes a bestseller and fans clamour for a sequel, you can pick up those threads, and it will feel like a natural development.

FURTHER STUDIES

You may want to explore novel plotting options with my book *Writing Vivid Plots.*

ASSIGNMENT

Decide what kind of ending you want for your novel, and what kind of emotion you want your reader to feel when she puts the book down after the final page.

Make these choices before you start plotting, writing or revising the scene.

CHAPTER 13

OUTDOOR SCENES

If your scene takes place outdoors, the location can enrich the plot. The characters may appear (or feel) small in the vast landscape, helpless, overwhelmed and lost. Nature — sometimes unpredictable, sometimes inevitable — shapes events.

Outdoor settings often work well for:

- Love scenes (for example, the doomed lovers meet on the windswept moor)

- Battles (for example, two medieval armies clash in the blistering desert heat)

- Quests (for example, the hero must find the hermit who lives in the forest)

- Explorations (for example, the archaeologists excavating an ancient temple)

- Searches (for example, the police team with dogs searching for a body in the woods)

- Climax scenes (for example, the hero and villain have a final showdown on the cliff edge)

WHAT'S THE WEATHER LIKE?

For an outdoors scene, make sure you involve the weather, and show how it affects the characters and the actions:

Which direction does the wind come from? How strong is it? What's the temperature like? Does the rain hit the PoV from the front or from behind? How does the weather affect the character

— does the hail sting her cheeks, is water sloshing in her shoes and creeping up her socks, does sweat trickle down her armpits?

WHAT DOES THE SKY LOOK LIKE?

Describe its colour — if possible in more imaginative ways than 'blue' or 'grey' and the pattern of clouds. Be creative, because descriptions of the sky can serve to establish the PoV's mood and may even foreshadow events.

WHERE'S THE SUN?

Where does the sun stand in the sky — in what direction, and how high? How sharp and how long are the shadows? How bright or sparse is the sunlight? What hue does the sunlight give to the surroundings — does it gild everything with a warm glow, does it create stark contrasts? Describe if something glints, gleams or sparkles in the light.

The location of the sun and the quality of the sunlight not only conjure atmosphere, but give clues to the season and the time of the day. In the morning, the light tends to be cool and clear, showing everything in bright colours with crisp outlines. Around noon and early afternoon, the light is intense and harsh, with very short shadows, and everything looks washed-out and pale. In the late afternoon, the light becomes softer, warmer, dipping everything in a golden glow, and the shadows lengthen. Sunset brings magnificent colour effects. (Note: these effects can vary depending on where in the world the story takes place).

WHAT'S THE GROUND LIKE?

Is the asphalt dotted white with seagull droppings, or black with old chewing gum? Are the paving-slabs cracked, lichen-encrusted or worn smooth? What sounds do the PoV's footsteps make? Is the lawn shorn short, or tangled with weeds? Is the ploughed field so soggy that clumps of clay soil attach themselves to the walker's boots, or is it baked hard in the dry heat?

In urban locations, what kind of rubbish lies on the ground — empty beer cans, used condoms, or apple cores? What kind of graffiti arc sprayed on the walls?

WHAT KIND OF PLANTS GROW?

What trees grow in the place? Pines, pears or poplars? Are they winter-bare, verdant with young leaves, laden with fruit, or gilded with autumn? Tall or dwarfing, sparse or lush, stunted from continued severe winds or crippled by an overzealous gardener's pruning shears?

How are the lawns and gardens kept? Do tulips stand in orderly rows, or do weeds choke the gardens? What are the weeds — brambles with their thorny tentacles, sycamore seedlings plotting to turn the garden into a dense wood in a few short years, or dandelions cheerfully resisting the gardener's strict regime?

WHAT SOUNDS ARE CREATED BY THE ENVIRONMENT?

Cars humming/roaring/whining past? Leaves rustling overhead? Twigs breaking as an unseen animal steps on them? The outdoors is never completely silent. If you want to emphasise a sense of silence, do it by describing a faraway noise (for example, the distant howl of a coyote).

WHAT ANIMALS CAN BE SEEN OR HEARD?

Mentioning an animal brings life to a scene. Is there a dog splashing in the brook, a cat lazing on the low wall, or an owl hooting in the distance? Perhaps a heavily-laden donkey plods past, or a horse clip-clops down the lane. Do birds twitter, chirp, screech?

WHAT DOES THE PLACE SMELL OF?

Outdoor scenes need smells, unless it is very cold. Smells are great at evoking a sense of the place, and a single sentence about smells achieves more than a whole paragraph of visual descriptions. What does the air smell of? Bonfire smoke? Lilies in bloom? Freshly mowed grass? Petrol fumes? The warmer the temperature, the more intense the smells.

HOW DO PEOPLE MOVE?

The weather and temperature affect the pace and purpose of movement — for your story's characters as well as for everyone else.

If it's cold, people move fast, with their hands in their pockets. They don't linger, and they avoid gestures. They don't do anything outdoors unless they have no choice. Individuals who have to spend time outdoors may rub their hands, stomp their feet or hug themselves for warmth.

If it's raining, they move fast, usually leaning forward, with their heads bent.

In warm weather, people linger. There may be groups milling about.

In hot weather, movements are slow, languid. People don't work outdoors unless they have no choice. Individuals may choose to hang out in the full sun, while many seek the shade of walls or trees.

NOVICE WRITER MISTAKES TO AVOID

New writers often write outdoor scenes without specific weather. The resulting scenes lack realism.

Another mistake is the so-called 'pathetic fallacy' where the writer chooses the weather to suit the MC's mood. When she cries, the clouds open and raindrops fall. When she's happy, the sun smiles.

To the reader, this feels clichéd and sentimental rather than realistic.

PROFESSIONAL TIP

Let your characters interact with their surroundings, even if it's only in small ways. Perhaps the MC steps around the puddles, takes careful steps to avoid slipping on the icy pavement, or picks blackberries growing along the footpath.

FURTHER STUDIES

The suggestions in this chapter are from my book *Writing Vivid Settings* which gives in-depth guidance on using and describing locations.

ASSIGNMENTS

1. For the outdoors scene you want to write or revise, decide the location, season, time of the day and weather. Write one sentence each about the sunlight, ground, sky, weather and temperature, to insert into the scene.

2. Go somewhere out of doors — take your dog for a walk in a municipal park, or sunbathe on the beach, or have a cup of tea in a pavement café — and observe the light, sounds, smells, wind, weather, ground and sky. Also, watch how people are moving. Jot down your observations and save them for use in either your current work-in-progress or a future story.

CHAPTER 14

INDOOR SCENES

Does the action of your novel sometimes play out indoors? Here are some suggestions to enhance those scenes.

1. Give the reader an idea how large the room is — not in yards and meters, but with creative descriptions and perhaps comparisons. Examples:

   The studio held a narrow bed, a chair and a bookcase, with little room to walk between them.

   His apartment was smaller than my garden shed.

   The kitchen sprawled across more space than my apartment.

   The villa's bathroom was nearly as big as the school's swimming pool.

2. Instead of describing everything, show a few telling details, such as the state of the houseplants (dried-up brown leaves? Flourishing lush green? Infested with blackfly and scale?) and the floor (wooden planks, bare concrete, a threadbare carpet, synthetic fleeces, ethnic rugs?)

3. Insert visual descriptions of the room in several places throughout the scene instead of all at the beginning. The PoV character who spends some time in this room will notice details bit by bit, as he looks around.

4. When the PoV gets bored with the conversation, you can indicate this by describing details of the interior. This implies that she's looking around instead of paying attention to what is being said.

5. The best place to insert smells is the moment the PoV enters the room, because the human brain perceives smells most

clearly when they're new. Mention a smell or combination of smells: cigarette smoke and unwashed socks, disinfectant and bleach, home-baked bread and beeswax, joss sticks and cannabis, hairspray and nail varnish remover. Smells create an immediate impression of the place and create an image in the reader's mind, even if you don't provide many visuals.

6. The furnishings and decor serve to reveal something about the person who chose them. How wealthy or poor is he? How orderly, tidy, clean, organised? Does she like stark simplicity or many knicknacks, old-fashioned cosy comforts or state-of-the-art functionality? The books on the shelf show the owner's taste. Mention a couple of titles. Does she read *Wuthering Heights, How To Lose Weight Fast, Kritik Der Reinen Vernunft,* or *Fifty Shades Of Grey?*

7. The decor can also hold subtle clues that will play a role later on in the story. By showing a shelf of shooting contest trophies, you signal that the guy who lives here is an expert marksman.

8. What kind of noises can the PoV hear while he is in the room? Perhaps there's a faint hum from a laptop, a steady tick-tock from the grandfather clock, a dripping water tap, footsteps from the flat above, and the flush and gurgle of the toilet on the other side of the wall. Insert noises whenever you want to emphasise tension, and also to indicate that the characters are not talking.

9. What's the weather like outside? This affects how the characters arrive. (Do they take off their muddy boots on entering, hang up their dripping coats, pull their chairs close to the radiator, clutch their cold-stiffened fingers around the coffee cups or gulp down ice-cold drinks?) The weather also provides interesting background noises, especially rain and wind.

10. What's the temperature like, and where does it come from? Is the room heated with a log fire, with a whirring fan heater, or with the old type of wall heater where the user has to insert

coins to keep it going? Does the room have air conditioning, or does a cooling draft come from the open windows? How comfortable is the temperature for the PoV?

11. How dim or well-lit is this room? Where does the light come from — large windows, candles, a ceiling lamp, or indirect lightning? Is it soft or harsh, warm or cold, bright or dim? Describing the colour, quality and source of light creates atmosphere. Mention the source of light early in the scene.

12. Indoors, people tend to be more relaxed, because they instinctively feel safer. They need not worry about animal predators, human muggers, or extreme weather. Show this in their body language and the way they interact. (Depending on the plot, don't give them the chance to relax for long, but expose them to tension and dangers).

13. Let the characters interact with their environment. This adds a sense of realism. For example, you can show how a character leans back in his chair, another perches on the edge of hers, a third pulls the chair closer to the fire. Someone may rearrange the tapestry cushions for comfort, while another wipes a spillage off the polished glass table. Unless they have met purely to talk or relax, give them some work to do. They may repair the floor, wash the dishes or search the attic for treasure.

14. Voices sound louder indoors than out of doors, because wind doesn't carry the sound away and there are fewer background noises.

15. For restaurant scenes, use description to make this an individual place, not a generic eatery. A sentence listing several smells establishes what kind of food they serve. Describe the surface of the tables — starched white linen, shiny metal, cracked plastic or scarred wood? How are the menus presented? Leather-bound books, laminated sheets sticky to the touch, or a chalkboard with spelling errors above the counter? What clothes do the servers wear — jeans and t-shirts, black dresses and lace-edged aprons,

or miniskirts and cleavage-baring tops? Include background noises — the hiss of the coffee maker, the rattling of cutlery, the bubbling of hot grease. If there's any music, mention the volume and style. You can also mention snatches of overheard conversations from the neighbouring tables.

16. If the scene takes place in a workspace, such as an office, workshop or factory, show the tools of the trade, preferably in motion. Mention smells. Almost every workplace has its characteristic smells — resin, leather, wax, grease, diesel, disinfectant, printer's ink, coffee. If work is under way, describe sounds — machines rattling, hammers clanking, printers whirring, monitors beeping.

17. For interesting plot developments, let one character discover an item that reveals a secret or exposes the owner's lie. Another way to add interest is if a character arrives late, perhaps someone nobody expected and nobody wants there, but courtesy forces them to tolerate this person's presence. Or consider a situation where the PoV character wants to leave the room, but can't.

18. If it suits your story, you can use the confined space to create a sense of claustrophobia in the PoV and the reader.

19. Indoor scenes lend themselves to 'locked room' mystery. Everyone can see everyone else, nobody leaves the room without being noticed. Yet, at the end of the scene, one of the characters is found murdered. Whodunnit?

NOVICE WRITER MISTAKES TO AVOID

New writers often vary between two extremes: either they use generic interiors (e.g. a bland living room that could be anyone's anywhere, without a clue about the inhabitant's lifestyles and personalities) or they over-load the description with information the reader doesn't need (e.g. the exact distance between the door and the couch, and every single colour in the carpet).

PROFESSIONAL TIP

Use the fact that the characters are indoors for subtle psychological manipulation of their — and the reader's — emotions.

When people gather indoors, they are typically closer together than outdoors, because the four walls keep them confined. It's not so easy to stroll away from an indoor gathering as outside. When a character leaves, everyone notices. People think twice about leaving, because they'll have to offer an excuse and say goodbye, thus drawing attention to themselves. This proximity can intensify tensions, something you can use in your dialogue.

Characters may stay together longer than they planned, because of conditions out of doors. Maybe they can't leave because there's a violent downpour, or the taxi doesn't come. This causes a shift in their emotions — perhaps frustration, impatience or embarrassment.

ASSIGNMENT

Imagine the room. Choose three objects which reveal something about the inhabitant's lifestyle or personality.

CHAPTER 15

NIGHT SCENES

Do you want a scene in your novel to be especially intense, emotional, creepy, scary, romantic or exciting?

Let it play out at night.

To create the right atmosphere, you need to trigger the reader's senses differently than for a daytime scene. In this post, I'll show you the techniques professional fiction authors use.

Use different senses. In the dark or semi-dark, your PoV character will see less than in bright light, so use the sense of vision less and the other senses more.

The sense of hearing is especially important. Insert several background noises, such as:

Outside, a car door slammed and a motor whined.

From the kitchen came the persistent drip-drop-drip of a leaking tap.

Water gurgled down the drainpipe.

Wind whispered through the branches and rustled the leaves.

Rain hammered on the window panes.

Insert sentences of this kind especially in moments of tense silence. They can help increase the suspense.

In the evening, most people's sense of smell heightens, so you may want to mention the scents and odours of the place and the characters. However, this awareness lessens in the early morning hours. The temperature also affects the sense of smell — during a balmy night, the characters will notice more smells than if it's cold.

Here are examples:

The rain sharpened the smells of smoke and earth.

He smelled of cigarettes and stale sweat.

She reeked of whisky and resentment.

Her scent was sweet, fruity, reminding him of the aroma of a freshly sliced peach.

The alley stank of rotting vegetables and piss.

From the entrance came the enticing smells of pizza and fried fish.

Any lights, whether nearby or faraway, will be noticeable at night, so mention lights. Here are some ideas for outdoor night scenes:

- car headlights
- street lamps (a row of them or a single one)
- lit windows in houses
- the glowing tip of a cigarette
- the stars (unless the sky is cloudy)
- neon advertising signs
- the moon (full, waxing, waning, crescent, gibbous)
- a campfire
- lanterns
- torches
- the hazy cloud of light above a distant city
- any appliances in use (a tablet, a mobile phone)

Describe the colour, quality and movement of the light. Use your full creativity to come up with original, atmospheric descriptions.

Here are some examples to inspire your own ideas:

Stars winked like sequins on a dark velvet gown.

Torches waved their yellow flames in the gloom.

The light of the lantern shuddered in the darkness.

The silvery sheet of the lake's surface darkened and lightened with every passing of a cloud.

Beams of light burst into the moonless night.

A pair of headlights sliced through the darkness.

The street lamps cast their sulphurous glow on the wet asphalt.

If the characters are indoors, your scene may be well-lit, but you can still show the source and quality of the light:

The overhead strip lights flickered to life.

The lamp cast its smoky light on the carpet.

The light bulb cast a pale glow, leaving the corners in shadow.

She relaxed in the generous glow of the clustered candles.

The log in the crate spluttered and fell apart, throwing orange sparks.

Artificial light affects how objects and people look. Candlelight tends to flatter the complexion, while white bulbs and neon tubes emphasise every wrinkle, blemish and scar. Use this effect in your descriptions.

To create a night-time atmosphere for your scene, also consider showing drawn curtains, or having your characters draw them against the approaching darkness.

If the scene takes place outdoors, show the weather and the temperature, the way your point-of-view character experiences them:

The night chill seeped through her jacket.

He tightened his hood and marched onwards through the battering storm.

Slivers of hail stung my cheeks.

Raindrops made needle streaks in the light of the street lamps.

Fear, danger, anxiety, uncertainty, are increased in the dark. By emphasising the darkness, you can create suspense and fear.

If you want to frighten your readers, give the point-of-view character light to see by at the beginning of the scene... and then take it away.

Here are some ideas on how to achieve this:

- One by one, the candles burn down.
- The wind blows out the lantern.
- Rain extinguishes the campfire, or the character runs out of wood to burn.
- A power cut drops the whole house into darkness.
- The battery runs out.

Try the effect of diminishing light for any scary or creepy scene in your novel. Your readers will shiver with delighted fear.

NOVICE WRITER MISTAKES TO AVOID

Beginner writers often fail to create a convincing night-time experience because they don't use the senses enough. Remember to use the senses of hearing, touch, smell and temperature, as well as other senses, such as taste, if relevant to the context.

PROFESSIONAL TIP

Experience the night, and use this for inspiration. Go out at night — ideally to a place that resembles a location in your WiP, or somewhere bizarre. If you dare, walk through a rough neighbourhood or visit the local graveyard at night. (Stay safe! Best take your dog or an understanding friend. If you don't want to leave your home after dark, your own back garden can yield interesting material, or you can simply throw a window open and lean out to listen, look and smell.) Absorb the lights, sounds and odours of the place. Collect as many observations as possible and write them down, for use in this scene and in future stories.

FURTHER STUDIES

To learn more about using the setting in your fiction, read *Writing Vivid Settings*.

ASSIGNMENTS

Imagine the location of your night scene. What smells might the PoV character notice? What noises can be heard in the background? Where does the light come from, and what's its colour, strength and effect? How does the ground feel underfoot? Write at least five sentences about the setting — as many of them as possible about a sense other than seeing — and sprinkle them throughout your scene.

CHAPTER 16

TRAVEL SCENES

Does your novel include a travel scene? Maybe the main characters are on a journey when the story begins or ends. Perhaps the novel's climax unfolds in a vehicle. A love scene might unfold on a yacht, a fight scene in a stage coach, or a scary scene in an underground train.

Here are some suggestions for making the journey a vibrant experience for your readers.

WHAT'S THE WEATHER LIKE?

'Nice' and 'normal' weather is dull. Instead, let the characters travel through a heat wave, heavy snow, brilliant sunshine, drizzling rain or howling wind. Tip: the more intense you make the weather, the more intense the scene becomes.

What's the temperature like? Are the characters sweating or shivering? What do they do to keep warm or to cool down? Do they pull their shawls tight around their shoulders and hug themselves for warmth, or do they fan themselves with newspapers and thirstily gulp water from plastic bottles?

Does the weather make them feel gloomy, faint or cranky? Does water drip from their coats and umbrellas, and form puddles on the carriage floor?

(You may want to re-read the chapters on 'Location and Weather' and 'Outdoor Scenes' for further ideas.)

SHOW THE LANDSCAPE

The walker has the time to observe the landscape in detail. The rider and motorist see it too, albeit at greater speed. Even the train traveller will gaze out of the window now and then.

Show the reader what the point-of-view character sees. Avoid lengthy descriptions. Instead, use a few brief words to evoke a clear image in the reader's mind: *Seagulls swooped from craggy cliffs. Waves ruffled the blue-grey lake. Cypress trees stood like sentinels, dark and straight.*

On long journeys, focus on how the landscape changes: *Pine-covered slopes gave way to sun-parched fields. The train left the stony heights and dived into lush meadows.*

LISTEN TO THE SOUNDS

Do the carriage wheels rattle or creak? Do the horse's hooves clip-clop or ping on the stone-flagged road? Do the PoV's boots thud on the asphalt, or does the gravel crunch under his feet? Does the car's motor hum, buzz, whine or roar? The train may whoosh along the track, or perhaps the steam engine pants up the mountain.

If you get the chance, experience the type of transport the PoV uses in your story, and pay attention to the sounds. If that's not practical, listen to sound clips, or use your memory or imagination.

THE POWER OF SMELL

The sense of smell is the most evocative sense. The moment you mention a smell, the reader becomes immersed in the experience. In a travel scene, let your reader get a whiff of the odours in the vehicle. The best moment for this is when the PoV gets in. When she enters the stage coach, does she notice smells of leather, sweat, pipe smoke and axel grease? When she squeezes into the crowded carriage on the London Piccadilly Line, does she get hit by stale air with odours of sweat, fish & chips and cheap perfume?

If the PoV travels on foot or on horseback, she will notice new smells whenever the landscape changes: the honey scent of buddleias in the suburban gardens, the tang of salt and seaweed along the ocean shore, the earthy aroma of pine resin in the forest.

COMFORT AND DISCOMFORT

How comfortable is your journeying character? She may travel first class with every comfort provided — but the scene may be more vivid if her buttocks hurt from the unaccustomed saddle, if her feet ache from marching in too-tight shoes, if she has to stand squeezed between strangers' bodies on a London Underground train, or if the camel's swaying gait makes her feel seasick.

FELLOW TRAVELLERS

Describe the people who share the carriage, bus, train compartment or camel caravan with the PoV. However, don't focus on any one passenger in particular, or describe anyone in detail, unless they play an active role in the scene or appear again in a later chapter. Instead, show just a brief glimpse: *Adolescent girls giggled over text messages. A tired-looking housewife clutched a bulging grocery bag.*

NOVICE WRITER MISTAKES TO AVOID

Don't write a travel scene unless something happens on the trip that affects the story. The journey itself is not a plot event. If the purpose of the trip is to get the character from A to B, simply sum it up in a few words *(After a gruelling four-day trip under the parching sun...)* and move on to the destination where the real events unfold.

Resist the temptation to turn the travel scene into an 'info-dump', using the journey to tell the reader everything about country's fauna, flora, history, politics or social conditions.

PROFESSIONAL TIP

Use the travel scene to pose challenges for the MC — not just obstacles he needs to overcome, but challenges that make him grow. By finding solutions to those challenges, he gains valuable experiences and becomes a wiser, more skilled and mature person.

ASSIGNMENTS

1. What important events play out during this scene? Write a brief outline of what happens (using the method shown in the chapter 'Plot Events') to decide whether this is genuinely a scene or could be cut.

2. Write a sentence describing the sounds the means of transport (horse, carriage, motorbike, whatever) makes.

CHAPTER 17

ARGUMENT SCENES

Dialogue scenes in which two characters argue are great for showing conflict and adding plot complications.

How do you write a great fictional argument? Here are fifteen professional techniques to make a confrontation sizzle.

1. Give the characters something to do while they argue, whether it's digging over the vegetable patch or knitting baby blankets, or better still, an activity that's crucial to the plot. The movements and sounds add interest to what would otherwise be a pure 'talking heads' section.

2. For best effect, force the quarrelling characters to work together as a team on a project. Perhaps they're tunnelling their way out of a dungeon, or abseiling down a steep cliff, and can only succeed by working as a team. Perhaps one isn't pulling his weight with the work, which irks the other and adds fuel to the verbal fight. On the other hand, if both work hard and operate as a team, relying on and trusting each other even as they argue, this adds poignancy and lays the groundwork to a meaningful relationship between the two.

3. Don't model the fiction scene too closely on real life arguments. In real life, people repeat the same points over and over. That would bore the reader. Instead, each character presents each point just once, in succinct, well-chosen words. If you allow a character to say the same thing three times, let the other counter with three different answers.

4. Keep the sentences tighter and shorter than in real life arguments.

5. Brief argument scenes are exciting, long ones dull. Keep it shorter than a real-life quarrel.

6. Characters may interrupt one another:

   "But Grandma said —"

   "Leave Grandma out of this!"

7. To tag dialogue, choose verbs which convey the tone of voice: *he spat, she yelled, he snapped, she screeched, he roared, she growled, he threatened.* But bear in mind that not every dialogue line needs a tag. If it's clear who's talking (or yelling), do without one. Also avoid tags with long verbs: *she vociferated, he expostulated.*

8. Use body language to convey the emotions. To express anger, show characters clenching fists and jaws, banging doors behind them, stomping, slamming hands onto tables. Use facial expressions and posture shifts. But bear in mind that characters aren't usually aware of their own body language. If you write the scene from one character's Point-of-View, show only the other person's facial expressions.

9. During the argument, the characters may grab, squeeze and clutch things. If things get heated, they may even throw or smash them.

10. Describe the speaker's voice, especially when the tone changes. Similes work especially well for this. Here are some examples:

    Her voice screeched like a dentist's drill.

    He growled like a chained Rottweiler.

    Her voice was as sharp as a gutting knife.

11. Consider each character's ranking in the hierarchy. For example, officer and grunt, teacher and student, boss and employee, king and subject, master and servant, high caste and low caste, older person and younger person (in cultures where age is revered), husband and wife (in societies where women are subservient to men). The higher-ranking person will remind his opponent

sharply of the difference. The lower-ranking character will be cautious not to cause offence — or if he does, it means he's deliberately challenging the other's authority, a huge risk.

12. One of the characters may say *"I told you so"* if they're talking about something that went wrong. *"How many times did I warn you about the icy steps? I told you someone would slip and fall. But did you listen?"*

13. Consider the location. The couple's living room may be the obvious place for a marital quarrel, and the office for a business conflict. Can you think of a setting that's less obvious, but still plausible in the context? This will add interest. Let the characters interact with their environment, to avoid the 'talking heads in white space' effect.

14. If the characters insult one another, invent creative insults. Instead of yelling *"You fucking son of a bitch!"* and *"You bloody bastard!"* they may shout *"You maggoty harbour rat!"* and *"You higgs-bosoned wormhole!"* Draw inspiration from the novel's setting and the characters' jobs, and have fun.

15. A clever character will ask leading questions — the kind that make the opponent trip up and say the wrong thing, a bit like a prosecution lawyer cross-examining a witness of the defence.

NOVICE WRITER MISTAKES TO AVOID

New writers often insert cuss words to emphasise the speaker's strong feelings, or in the mistaken belief that this creates realism.

The effect is often the opposite of what these writers intend.

In real life, many people cuss a lot — but this doesn't mean you have to replicate this in fiction. You may want to keep the language in your novel clean. Even if you decide to include cussing, think carefully about when and how much to allow. A whole scene in the style of *"You fucking idiot, why did you fucking have to fucking do this. I fucking told you to fucking leave this alone!"* may be realistic — but dull.

In a fictional argument, the reader gets the impression that the character who cusses has the weaker arguments. This person comes across as needing to bolster his feeble reasoning with swearing. So instead of emphasising what the character says, the cuss words actually weaken his statements.

PROFESSIONAL TIP

Cussing can make a character's position and reasoning appear weak. Consider using this psychological effect in your argument scene. When one of the characters uses more and more swearwords, it signals to the reader that the cusser is losing the argument and knows it.

Let's say two war leaders argue over who should hold a fortress. Each presents his points and argues his position, and, at first, they use similar language. Then one resorts to swearing.

Here are two variations. Observe how you, as the reader, perceive what they say.

Version 1:

"In this case, you don't need the fortress and can surrender it."

"I won't fucking surrender the fucking fortress. It's my fucking right to stay."

Version 2:

"Then you don't fucking need the fucking fortress and can fucking surrender it."

"I won't surrender the fortress. It's my right to stay."

The reader will respect and root for the character who does not cuss — simply because he appears more reasonable, intelligent and confident.

FURTHER STUDIES

For a wealth of professional dialogue techniques, consult *Writing Vivid Dialogue* in the Writer's Craft series.

ASSIGNMENTS

Decide which of the suggested techniques you want to use in your scene. You don't have to use them all.

Now write a section of the dialogue in which each character gets to speak twice. (Character A says something, then Character B, then A again, then B.) Write it so that each makes their points as clearly and tightly as possible. Include at least one body language clue to convey emotion or attitude.

CHAPTER 18

CONFESSION SCENES

When one character makes a confession to another, the emotional stakes are high. How will the other react? How does this affect the relationship between those two characters? It may even turn the listener's whole world upside down.

My suggestions apply to any gender, although for readability I'll assume that the confessing character is male, and the recipient of the confession female.

WHAT TO CONFESS?

He must tell her the truth about something that he has hidden or lied about until now. Here are some examples:

- The husband confesses to his wife that he had an affair with his assistant.

- The bridegroom confesses to his bride that he already has a wife.

- The father confesses to his daughter that she is not really his child.

- The employee confesses to his boss that he faked his references and has neither the qualifications nor the skills he claimed.

- He confesses to the police officer that he committed the serial killings for which an innocent man was executed.

- He isn't the person he claimed to be.

- The husband confesses to his wife that he only married her for her money.

- It was he who stole the jewels — a crime for which her brother was hanged.

- He confesses to her daughter that he has just sold her as a slave. (In some historical societies, a father had the right to sell his offspring.)

- He has gambled away the money she lent him to invest.

These are, of course, extreme examples. Other confessions may be relatively minor, but those won't require a full scene for themselves. You can incorporate minor confessions into another scene, using the same techniques but toning them down.

WHY IS THIS CONFESSION SO DIFFICULT?

Make it as difficult as possible for him to tell her the truth. He knows that the truth will hurt her, that it will change their relationship, that it will destroy her trust in him, that he may lose her love, that she may leave him, disinherit him or report him to the police.

That's why he kept the truth from her for so long.

Why is this truth so devastating for her? Create several reasons, and make them as intense as possible, so the truth is unbearable.

Let's take one example: A husband confesses to his wife that her miscarriage wasn't an accident, but arranged by him. That is shocking and devastating enough — but you can make it worse. What if as the result of the miscarriage, she can never become pregnant again? What if this was her only chance of ever having a child? What if her childlessness makes her an outcast in a society where a woman's worth depends on motherhood? What if she had loved that unborn child like she had never loved anything or anyone? What if that child, if born, had secured the succession to the throne and prevented the devastating war that cost thousands of lives? What if he is the figurehead of an anti-abortion campaign, and must now reveal himself as a hypocrite? What if he swore an oath — perhaps on his wife's life — that it was an accident, and now he must admit that the oath was false? What if an innocent person got punished for causing the miscarriage?

Pile it on, and make it as awful as you can.

WHY IS HE TELLING IT NOW?

He hid the truth for a long time. The longer he kept the secret, the more difficult it became to confess.

So why does he confess now? There must be a reason for the timing. Here are some ideas:

- Someone else is going to tell her, and he wants her to hear the truth from him, not anyone else.

- He is getting blackmailed.

- They're about to enter a new stage in their relationship — for example, they're getting married and he wants her to know the truth before she commits.

- He fears that she is about to discover the truth.

- He is suspected of a horrible crime that carries the death penalty, the only way to prove his innocence is to provide an alibi for that night — which requires him to come clean about where and with whom he had spent the night.

- He wants to prevent an innocent person going to prison for the crimes he committed.

- He has embraced religion, and his new faith requires him to confess his sins.

- He is dying, and wants to tell the truth while he still can.

- He has changed, and become more honest and courageous.

HOW DOES HE TALK?

Be aware of his emotions. What does he feel? What does he expect will happen? What outcome does he hope for? What outcome does he fear? How does he rally-up=the courage to finally speak the truth?

In this type of scene, body language (posture, movement, gestures, facial expressions, tone of voice, visceral responses) creates reader emotion.

Describe the character's voice as he confesses — does he stutter, speak in a low voice, or talk fast to get it over with?

How does he stand or sit? How does he move? Does he look at her while he confesses, or at the floor? What does he do with his hands?

To get his approach, voice and body language right, consider what he feels. He probably feels several different emotions during the scene such as nervousness, fear, determination, guilt, embarrassment, shame, regret and remorse.

HOW DOES SHE REACT?

Arrange it so the confession has an emotional impact on her. She doesn't just nod and take notes. Instead, she is shocked and shaken to hear the truth. She struggles to process the information, and needs time to form an opinion and decide what to do.

During this scene, she will experience a vast range of intense emotions. These may include: apprehension, dread, confusion, shock, disgust, hatred, hurt, insecurity, disbelief, fear, jealousy, fury, resentment, hopelessness, resignation, depression, sadness, grief, unhappiness, despair.

If you write the scene from the confession recipient's PoV, let the reader feel her visceral reactions. If the scene is in the confessing character's PoV, show the other person's body language.

Her reaction will come in stages, as she processes what he has told her. Her first response probably doesn't reflect her final assessment and decision. Indeed, she may need several days to absorb the enormity of what happened, and to come to terms with it one way or another.

HOW TO END THIS SCENE

If the two characters are in a personal relationship, e.g. husband and wife, father and daughter, siblings, lovers or friends, a good way to close this scene is with the confession-receiver sending the confession-giver away. This is realistic. It can express her anger (*"Get out of my sight!"*), confusion (*"Please go. I need to be alone"*), or any other emotion. It also keeps the emotional tension high.

If you use the 'scene & sequel' method of scene structuring, this ending will sequel neatly into a 'sequel' section in which the PoV character reflects, processes and plans.

On the other hand, if the confession-recipient has listened in a professional capacity (i.e. as a police officer, employer, judge or priest), the scene probably closes with the professional taking the appropriate action — arrest, formal dismissal from the job, sentencing or absolution.)

HOW DOES THE RELATIONSHIP CHANGE?

If the two characters had a personal connection before (being for example friends, colleagues, spouses, siblings or lovers) the relationship between the two will never be the same again.

Even if she keeps his secret, she will not feel the same about him. Now that the confessing character's true role or identity is revealed, it affects who he is to her and how she treats him. Even more importantly, he has broken her trust by lying to her continuously. She won't be able to trust him again completely, not for a long time. From now on, she will be wary of anything he says, claims or promises.

The relationship changes the moment the truth is out, and it will continue to change over the next scenes, as both characters come to terms with what happened, and learn to trust again. It is possible that for the next days, weeks or months he is on 'probation' before she decides whether or not to forgive him.

In the long term, the relationship may become stronger, because it is now based on honesty, and because there is now genuine understanding between them.

But the relationship may not survive. When she finds out the terrible thing he's done, and realises how he has deceived her and that everything between them was based on a lie, she may break off the engagement or disinherit him. However much she loves him, she will sooner or later come to realise that the person she loved existed only in her wishful imagination, and that the real person does not deserve her trust.

Of course, these developments may not transpire until later in the novel, but you should lay the groundwork for them in this scene.

NOVICE WRITER MISTAKES TO AVOID

The recipient of the confession shouldn't immediately forgive. That's unrealistic, and it misses a great opportunity for emotional drama.

PROFESSIONAL TIP

The scene is a turning point in the plot, and it is potentially one of the most emotionally tense scenes in the novel. Plan the emotions (the characters', and the readers') carefully, and apply your craft skills to creating those feelings.

FURTHER STUDIES

To convey the characters' feelings, and to stir the readers' emotions, you may find my book *Writing Vivid Emotions* helpful.

ASSIGNMENTS

1. Why did the character in our story harbour this secret for so long? Why is it such a terrible thing to confess? Why does he choose this moment to confess? What emotions does he feel in this scene? Select several visible body language clues or visceral responses to convey these emotions.

2. Why is this revelation so devastating for the character who receives the confession? What hope and beliefs does this shatter in her? What emotions does she feel in this scene? Select several visible body language clues or visceral responses to convey these emotions.

3. How does the scene end?

CHAPTER 19

CREEPY SCENES

Do you want to write a ghost story? Are you working on a Thriller, an Urban Fantasy, a Paranormal Romance or a Horror novel? Then you need to create at least one creepy scene. Give your readers the spooky, spine-tingling experience they enjoy.

Try these six professional techniques.

USE SOUND EFFECTS

Weave many noises into your writing. Here are some ideas.

Voices

How do the voices sound?

Examples:

Her voice screeched like a rusty hinge.

He had the throaty voice of a heavy smoker.

Her voice had the shrill persistence of a dentist's drill.

His voice rumbled like thunder.

If you place this descriptive sentence immediately after the spoken line, you don't need to add 'he/she said.'

Action Sounds

Almost everything a character does creates a noise, either directly or indirectly. The great thing about action sounds is that the description won't slow the pace, so you can use them even in fast-paced scenes.

Examples:

Her footsteps whispered across the sand.

The door clicked back into the lock.

The bunch of keys in his hands rattled.

A floorboard creaked under my feet.

Background noises

Sounds unrelated to the action slow the pace but increase the suspense. This is perfect for situations where the main character is waiting for something. What's the weather like? This may yield atmospheric details.

Examples:

In the distance, a coyote howled.

Keyboards clacked, printers whirred and papers rustled.

Wind banged the doors and rattled the shutters.

Rain hammered against the window panes.

SHOW THE CREEPY CREATURE'S HANDS

When describing a monster, a villain or creepy person, find an opportunity to describe their hands or paws. Are they tanned or pale, pudgy or bony, scarred, calloused, grimy or carefully manicured?

If the point of view character experiences their touch, do the hands feel cool or hot, dry or sweaty, soft or rough? Describe the fingernails: long or short, chipped, nicotine-stained, with a shiny pink varnish or with black rims?

In the case of an animal or monster, are the paws leathery, hairy or covered in iridescent scales? Are the talons dagger-straight or curved like scimitars? Are they matte like tarnished copper, or do they shine like polished steel?

DARKNESS, LIGHT AND SHADOW

Set the scene in a dark or semi-dark place. It's a deep-seated human instinct to be nervous in the dark, and as writers, we can play with that. Perhaps you can choose a dark location, such as a forest at night or an unlit cave. You could also let the camp-fire burn down, the torch battery go flat, a power cut turn off all the lights, or the wind blow out the candle. Darkness reduces the vision. The character will hear, smell and feel more than usual, and this increases the creepiness and suspense.

Describe the source and quality of the light.

Where does the light come from, and what does it look like?

Examples:

The window slit admitted a mere sliver of light.

Moonlight painted the landscape in eerie silver.

Blinding light shot through the opening in the roof and painted a sharp rectangle on the carpet. Weak light filtered through the grime-streaked glass pane.

A bare bulb overhead threw a puddle of harsh light on the concrete floor.

The street lamps washed the road in their sulphurous glow.

The horizon shimmered crimson in the wash of the setting sun.

Let the lights move.

Moving, flickering, disappearing and reappearing lights add to a spooky effect. Describe the way the candle flickers or the way clouds ghost across the moon.

Examples:

The door opened, and the candle flames flickered.

Torches waved their yellow flames in the gloom.

The overhead neon tube cast a harsh, flickering light.

Flames rose and fell.

Lanterns danced along the path.

Show shadows.

Shadows add a wonderful layer of creepiness to any scene. Close your eyes, visualise the place, identify the shadows and include them.

Examples:

Shadows lengthened and crept like tentacles across the yard.

Grey shadows danced along the stone wall.

In the light of the candle, his writing hand cast a faint shadow on the sheet.

ENTER THROUGH A DOOR

To ratchet up the suspense, let the character enter through a door on the way to danger. To the reader's subconscious, this represents a final barrier, the last chance to stay safe. Describe the door in one or several sentences — for example, its appearance, how the doorknob feels in the character's palm, and the sound when it opens.

Examples:

The door's white paint was flaking, revealing previous coats of crimson and grey.

'Strictly No Entry. Danger Zone,' the sign on the door warned.

The knob of the doorbell was sticky with grime.

The double door had cracked glass panels and chipped black paint, plastered with notices for last year's events.

Keys rattled, the lock squealed, and the door opened.

She clasped the icy handle and pressed it down.

The door whined inwards on its hinges.

USE 'EE' AND 'S' SOUNDS

This is an advanced technique, highly effective especially for audiobooks and public performances, for instance, when you read out your story at a Halloween event.

Certain sounds create certain effects in the reader's subconscious. This is called 'euphonics.'

- To create a creepy impression, use words containing the 'EE' sound. In the English language, many words with a creepy meaning actually have that sound: *creep, scream, fear, squeal, screech, deep, steep.* You can enhance this effect by adding non-creepy words with that sound, such as *sleep, sheep, keep, peer, steer, hear, need, near.*

- The 'S' sound adds a hint of spookiness. It's already contained in may spooky words, such as *whisper, spook, ghost, spirit, silence, mystery, mist, secret, slither, sinister.* Add some other 'S' sounds to make it spookier still: *stand, steal, stones, sing, sit, crest, base.*

Just changing a few words to incorporate those sounds can add a subtle layer of creepy spookiness to your scene. For example, if your character takes a quick look, tweak a few words to let her *steal a peak* instead. Instead of walking quietly, she *sneaks* along the path, and the illumination comes not simply from moonlight but from the *crescent sliver* of the moon.

CHILL THE TEMPERATURE

Give the main character physical chills, and the reader's subconscious will shiver. Here are some possibilities: the fuel runs out, the camp fire burns down, night falls, the wind picks up. Maybe the action takes place in a cool cellar, a cave, an underground temple or an unheated attic. Perhaps the character is unprepared for the weather or the location, and wears too-thin clothes. Or maybe she's wet or exposed to the elements. Show how the cold feels to the character, and what she does about it.

Examples:

She pulled her cloak tighter around her shivering frame.

The wall felt icy to her touch.

The cold seeped through the thin soles of her sandals.

She rubbed her stiffening fingers against the encroaching cold.

They huddled closer to the fire, seeking warmth.

NOVICE WRITER MISTAKES TO AVOID

Beginners often tell readers that the experience is creepy: *The building was creepy. The clouds whisping across the moon had a creepy effect.*

It's much better if the reader thinks, "Oh, that is creepy!"

PROFESSIONAL TIP

I recommend using at least three of these techniques in your scene, selecting the ones that work best for your plot and writing style. Don't rely on a single technique, but layer them. You will find that each supports the others, for example, darkness also brings chills and more emphasis on sounds.

FURTHER STUDIES

My book *Writing Scary Scenes* contains many useful techniques for writers of creepy fiction.

ASSIGNMENT

Decide which of the above techniques you want to use in your scene.

Now write one descriptive sentence using each of those techniques, to insert into different sections of the scene.

CHAPTER 20

SCARY SCENES

How much do you want to frighten your readers in your novel's scariest scene? Consider what your readers expect.

Readers of Thrillers and Horror novels want to be terrified. They love a scene that makes their heart race and the knees quake, that constrict the throat so they can barely breathe, and turns their insides to water. Romance readers, on the other hand, like gentler frights that give them a thumping heart, a tingling scalp, perhaps a shudder or a gasp.

Some novels have several scary scenes, others may have only one, probably in the book's Black Moment or Climax section.

How do you frighten your readers? Here are some techniques for you to try, all perfect for giving your readers a spine-tingling, bone-chilling experience. Play with them, mix, match and adapt them to suit your genre, your author voice and your plot.

DIP THE SCENE IN DARKNESS

For humans, everything is more frightening when they can't see much in the dark. Can your scene take place at night, in a windowless room, a cave or mineshaft? The setting may be lit at the beginning of the scene. Then a gust of wind blows out the candle flame, a power cut shuts down the electric light, or a bullet shatters the single light-bulb.

Semi-darkness can also be effective: a single lantern at night, falling dusk, a heavily curtained window, torches on the dungeon walls, a thick canopy of trees blocking the sun. You can create creepy effects by showing the movement and variations of the light — the lantern sways in the wind, the candle flame flickers, clouds waft across the moon and shadows dance across the walls.

To increase the creepiness and fright, let the darkness increase gradually. The camp fire subsides. The hearth fire dies down. Night falls. Clouds thicken, blocking out the light of the moon. The candles burn down, one by one.

If your novel has several scary scenes, don't place them all in darkness, or the effect may be boring instead of thrilling.

GET VISCERAL

Fear affects the body. Describe these physical effects. If you let the readers feel the Point-of-View characters' physical reactions, they will feel the same.

Insert sentences like these:

Her heart thudded louder and louder.

His skin crawled.

Tendrils of terror curled into his stomach.

Cold sweat trickled down my sides.

My scalp prickled and her breath stalled.

Fear clogged his throat.

Her pulse pounded in her ears.

Cold sweat glued the shirt to his back.

Chills chased up her spine.

A ball of terror formed in his stomach.

Her stomach knotted.

A weight seemed to press on my chest, robbing me of breath.

Fear clenched like a tight first around my chest.

These sentences work better than 'He felt afraid' and 'She was extremely frightened.'

ADD SOUND EFFECTS

Of all the senses, the sense of hearing serves best to create excitement and fear. You can make any scene more frightening by inserting some sound effects. These sounds may be related to the plot and the characters' actions, or they can simply be background noises.

Here are some ideas:

The villain's boots clack on the floor tiles.

Water drips from the ceiling.

The dentist's drill whines.

The knife scrapes on the whetstone.

A faraway siren wails.

The wall clock ticks.

A dog barks outside.

An owl hoots.

The Point-of-View characters' own heartbeat thuds in his hears.

In suspenseful moments, you can ratchet up the tension even higher by inserting background noises.

During moments of fast action, don't describe far-away background noises. The PoV character would not be aware of them. You can, however, use action sounds, such as swords clanking during a duel and soles slapping on asphalt while the characters run.

OPEN A DOOR

To increase the suspense, put a door between the main character and the danger. If he has to open the door to enter, this creates a psychological barrier and presents his final chance to turn back.

Any kind of 'door' can serve: a front door, an entry arch, a trap door, garden gate, a stile, a cave mouth. Slow the pace by describing the door and how it opens. As always, sounds are effective. Insert a sentence or even a whole paragraph about the 'door' moment. Here are some phrases for your inspiration:

The door knob felt icy in my palm.

She fumbled in her bag for the keys.

The door's pink paint was flaking, revealing previous coats of crimson and black.

The knobs of the two doorbells were sticky with grime.

'Strictly No Entry. Danger Zone', the sign on the door warned.

The double door had cracked glass panels and chipped blue paint, plastered with notices for last year's special offers.

While he waited, steps shuffled inside, and then a key scraped in the lock.

The door swished open.

The door opened with a squeal.

The door whined inwards on its hinges.

The door rattled open.

To make the reader sit on the edge of her seat with tension and suspense, you can take this technique a step further. Show how the door closes behind the character. This creates the subliminal suggestion that the character is trapped.

Behind, her, the door snapped shut.

The door closed with a thud.

Don't use the 'door' effect for minor plot events. If you build suspense by pausing at the kitchen door, and all the character does is brew a cup of tea, the readers will feel cheated.

DROP THE TEMPERATURE

If the temperature drops, the fear factor rises. Make it uncomfortably cold for the main character, and the readers will shiver with her.

This technique works well in combination with the 'darkness' method, because dark places are often cold. The power-cut which switched off the lights stops the heating, too. Nightfall brings colder temperature with the darkness.

Here are some ideas for how to create a cold setting:

Perhaps it's winter, or evening, or perhaps a cool breeze chills everything. Maybe the owner of the place has turned the heating off to save energy, or maybe the survivors have run out of fuel, or perhaps the ceiling fan is over-active. Stone buildings, caves, and subterranean chambers tend to be cold.

Describe how the cold feels to the protagonist, how her skin pimples, how she rubs her arms to get warm, how her fingertips turn blue, how she shivers.

For the best effect, lower the temperature gradually. Perhaps it gets colder and colder as the weather gets worse, as fuel gets sparser, or as the main character crawls deeper into the catacomb.

Use the temperature-dropping effect only once or twice in your novel. If you over-use it, it loses its effectiveness.

DESCRIBE THE SCARY PERSON'S VOICE

When the villain, torturer, executioner, serial killer or concentration camp commander talks, describe his voice.

Similes (comparing the voice to another sound) work well, especially if the comparison is something dangerous from the Point-of-View character's range of experience. Does it remind the PoV of fingernails scraping on a blackboard, a strict teacher, wind howling in a chimney, grinding metal, a hypnotist, an unoiled hinge or a Rottweiler's growl?

Here are some examplesof how I've used this technique in my own fiction. Obviously, your style will be different, but these may serve as inspiration:

His voice had a sharp edge. (Druid Stones)

Baryush spoke with the sonorous tone of a satisfied customer. (Storm Dancer)

His voice softened to the texture of rubber. (Storm Dancer)

Kirral's voice had the soft scraping tone of a sword grinding against a whetstone. (Storm Dancer)

His voice had the low-humming hiss of a wasp hovering over rotting fruit. (Storm Dancer)

He intoned an invocation of the Red Goddess, his voice deep and resonant, like that of the solo baritone in Kathy's church choir. (Druid Stones)

... he says in his soft singsong voice. (Beltane)

His voice is deep and brisk. (Beltane)

Dirk's voice was heavy with importance, reminding us that underlings must follow their leader. (I Dived the Pandora)

Dirk lectured in his preacher's voice. (I Dived The Pandora)

Her voice whined like a dentist's drill, shrill, painful, persistent. (Seagulls)

...he assured her, using the same tone as a dentist telling a patient it would hurt just a little. (Druid Stones)

You can apply this technique several times during the novel, but I wouldn't use it more than once or twice in each scene.

NOVICE WRITER MISTAKES TO AVOID

Newbies tend to tell the reader that a character feels fear: *She was afraid. He felt frightened.*

Once they discover how to show fear with visceral reactions, they go overboard with them, and insert visceral responses at the slightest trigger. If a character shudders whenever a door bangs and winces at every creaking of a floorboard, the readers will think the character is a wimp. It's better to reserve the viscerals for the really frightening moments.

PROFESSIONAL TIP

Combine three or more of these techniques in your scene, either simultaneously, or one after the other. It's also effective to start with one of them, then add the others gradually.

FURTHER STUDIES

You may want to study the techniques from the previous chapter, since 'scary' often overlaps with 'creepy.'

My book *Writing Scary Scenes* contains detailed advice for the suggestions I've offered here, as well as other techniques.

ASSIGNMENT

Choose the techniques you want to apply. With each technique, write one sentence or paragraph for your scene.

CHAPTER 21

MAGIC SCENES

Does your story have a mage, a wizard, a sorcerer or a witch cast a spell? Here are some tips for how to make this scene believable and exciting.

THE STRUCTURE OF THE RITUAL

Each act of magic requires a ritual. The details vary, depending on the magician's skill level and preferences, and the system of magic, but broadly it covers eleven steps. You want to structure your scene along the stages of the ritual, or show only some of the steps and gloss over others.

1. **Preparation**

   The mage locks the door, reads the instructions, gets his tools ready, assembles the ingredients, dons his robe, lights the candles.

2. **Circle-Casting**

   The mage now creates a circle. This can be a physical circle (for example, drawn with a finger in the sand or with chalk on the floorboards) or a mental one (visualised in her mind). The circle serves two purposes. It keeps harmful influences (e.g. dangerous demons attracted by the ritual) out, and it keeps the magic power in.

3. **Invocation**

   The mage prays to his god or goddess or a saint of his religion, summons a demon, calls nature spirits or invites the spirits of his ancestors, with a request that they lend a helping hand. Some mages will make an offering to the spirits they invoke, for example, pouring wine on the ground or — for darker kinds of magic — a bowl of blood to welcome the demon.

4. **Altering the State of Consciousness**

The magician changes how her brain functions so it becomes receptive to magic. Often, this involves going into a trance, for example through chanting, drumming or dancing. Deep meditation is also a possibility. Some mages take mind-altering drugs as a short-cut, while others consider that wrong.

5. **Raising Power**

Magic needs energy, and the magician either taps into an energy source or creates energy. This is an important phase of the ritual; without it, magic will not work. If you like, you can add sensory effects here, such as flickering lights, sounds, and changes in temperature. Readers enjoy these details.

6. **Speaking the Spell**

The mage speaks or chants the words of the spell. In some magic systems (such as Ancient Egyptian magic), it's essential to get the words, pronunciations and intonations exactly right. In others (such as Wiccan witchcraft) the words are merely a vehicle by which the spell travels, and what matters is the intent, i.e. the magician needs to concentrate fully on the purpose of the spell.

7. **Thanking or Dismissing the Spirits**

Once the spell is cast, the mage thanks the spirits for their assistance (if she invited them) or dismisses them (if she summoned them) or says another prayer to her goddess or god.

8. **Closing the Circle**

The mage dismantles the physical circle (for example, by wiping away the chalk line) or visualises the imaginary circle as fading.

9. **Grounding**

The mage needs to come back to reality. The quickest and easiest is to drink some water or eat a little bread.

10. **Keeping Records**

Like a scientist conducting experiments, the mage records what exactly he did during the ritual, with which ingredients, what the purpose was, how it felt, and so on. This allows him to keep track of the efficacy of the magic, and learn for future rituals.

11. **Resting**

Magic is mentally, emotionally and physically exhausting. After working major magic, the mage needs a rest. If possible, she'll take a nap.

Variations

Steps 2, 3, 4 and 5 are sometimes carried out in a different order or combined. For example, by drumming and dancing, the mage can change her consciousness and raise power at the same time.

The ritual can take as little as two seconds, or as long as two days. A public ritual is likely to take longer than a private one, because the mage wants to please the audience.

An experienced magician may use a shorter ritual than an inexperienced one. Ritual helps the magic, and a novice needs all the help she can get. An inexperienced magician gets the best results if she adheres to the ritual precisely and takes a lot of time. A veteran mage can do something in minutes or seconds because she has the experience.

PLOT IDEAS

In fiction, magic should not go smoothly. As with everything else, obstacles and mistakes make things interesting. Here are some ideas for how you can create twists to keep your scene exciting.

What if the mage doesn't have her accustomed tools and ingredients at hand, because she needs to work magic at short notice? Perhaps she doesn't even have enough to time to carry out the ritual properly.

What if her method of casting the circle takes time, but she is in a hurry, because an evil entity or human enemy is trying to invade? She'll have to finish the circle fast so she can be safe inside.

What if she requests the help of a spirit, and that spirit refuses to support the spell?

What if he summons a demon he has never worked with before, and that demon is too powerful for him to control?

What if tiredness or distractions make it impossible for her to concentrate, and she can't hold the intent in her mind?

What if he's mentally exhausted after the ritual, and his enemies use his vulnerability to attack?

You can also twist some of these ideas for a different perspective. If the good guys in your story seek to combat an evil sorcerer, they may try to distract him while he focuses on the spell's intent, or to attack the normally invincible mage during the short window of vulnerability after the magic spell.

NOVICE WRITER MISTAKES TO AVOID

Inexperienced writers — especially those who don't understand magic — tend to assume that all it takes is the mage pointing a wand and saying a secret word. That's unrealistic as well as unexciting.

PROFESSIONAL TIP

If the MC needs the magic spell to work (his scene goal), then let things go wrong, so the outcome remains uncertain until the end: a crucial ingredient is missing, the mage gets distracted and loses his concentration for a moment, a tool drops from his hand and falls outside the circle, the invoked entity doesn't accept the offering... Use your imagination to let things go wrong.

FURTHER STUDIES

If you're a Fantasy or Paranormal novelist, you'll find a wealth of suggestions in my book *Writing About Magic*.

ASSIGNMENT

Plan the magic ritual the way it is meant to be carried out, e.g. how the mage alters his consciousness, how he raises power, how he grounds after the ritual.

Now force the mage character to cope with less-than-ideal circumstances. How does he adapt the ritual? What problems arise?

CHAPTER 22

CAPTIVITY SCENES

Many novels feature at least one scene in which a character is locked up against her will. Perhaps she's been arrested, abducted or thrown into a dungeon, or maybe she's visiting a loved one in prison.

Here are some techniques to make this scene powerful.

FROM THE CAPTIVE'S POINT OF VIEW

If the reader experiences the scene from the perspective of the prisoner, consider the following suggestions.

1. Describe the sound as the cell door closes. Does it clank, screech or thud shut? Let the reader hear the related noises as well, such as rattling of keys in the lock and the thudding of boots as the jailer walks away.

2. If possible, make the room dark or semi-dark. This is creepier and can be unnerving for the reader as well as the character. Show how scarce the light is — the narrow rectangle of light falling through the high up window slit, the flickering torch.

3. During the character's first moments in the cell, describe what the place smells like. Olfactory impressions are strongest at the beginning. After a while, the mind gets used to them and they are no longer noticeable, so mention the stinks when the character does, which is the moment she enters that room.

Here are some ideas for unpleasant smells:

- Sour stench of urine

- Excrement from previous prisoners

- Old sweat

- Blood

- Rodent excrement

- Rotten straw

- Mould

- Food

4. Solitary confinement is scariest. If your character is alone in that room, with nobody to talk to, the reader worries for her. She may shout "Is anyone out there? Can you hear me?" and get no reply. Alternatively, she may have a companion in her captivity — until that person gets led away for execution. If several people are confined in a closed space — cell mates, or Jews transported in railway carriages to a death camp — describe body odours, movements, overheard snatches of conversation, snores, habits.

5. The place is probably cold, and you may want to make it very chilly indeed. This is plausible even in warm climates, because cells tend to be underground or behind thick stone walls. The place is unheated, the protagonist is not wearing many clothes, the air is chilly, the concrete floor is cold, and if a blanket is provided at all it is much too thin.

6. Use sounds. Sounds create unease and fear in the reader's subconscious — perfect for this type of scene. Here are some ideas:

- Rodents' feet

- Shuffling straw

- Fellow captives' sobs and snores

- Agonised screams from another cell

- Clanking doors, rattling keys, screeching locks

- Guard's boots thudding in the corridor Innocuous noises coming from outside

7. Mention how something feels to the touch. This works especially well if the place is dark.

   Ideas:

   - The fetters/handcuffs/bonds chafing at the wrists/ankles

   - Pain from bruises

   - The texture of the wall

   - Texture of the door

   - Cold hard floor

   - Rough blanket

   - Cobwebs

   - Sodden straw

   - Chilly air

8. Perhaps you can involve the sense of taste as well. What does the food taste like? The water? However, this may not be appropriate for all captivity scenes. The perception of taste also depends on how hungry and thirsty the prisoner is. At first, he may find the gruel and brackish water revolting, but after a while, he's so starved and parched, he'll devour and swallow what he can get.

   If the villain has gagged him, you can also describe how the gag tastes.

9. The captive examines the place, looking for ways to escape. This is a natural response to captivity, especially during the first

few hours. It's also a good way to show the reader how secure the prison is. Describe how strong the wall is, how high up and narrow the windows are placed, how several locks secure the door, with two jailers standing guard.

10. The pace in captivity scenes is slow, because the character is condemned to inactivity. Use this part of your novel to share the character's thoughts with the reader. She may reflect on her mistakes, gain insights and grow wiser. But don't allow the character to wallow in despair. Although she may feel dejected, she doesn't give up.

11. The captive has a sliver of hope that he might escape. This hope keeps the tension alive. Let him hope and plan. Later, the plan will probably fail, but it's important to show some hope in order to create suspense.

FROM THE VISITOR'S POINT OF VIEW

If the character is visiting the captive in prison, or rescuing her from her confinement, his immediate attention won't be on the place, but on the person of the captive. Does she look pale or healthy? Emaciated or strong? Does her voice sound feeble, dejected or defiant?

He will take in the surroundings, but not in great depth, because unlike the prisoner, the visitor doesn't have the time.

He will notice the smells the moment he enters the cell. Other senses will come into play as well, but only briefly.

FROM THE JAILER'S POINT OF VIEW

A kidnapper, prison guard or torturer will also observe the captive more than the place.

The place is familiar to him, so he no longer pays much attention. He's unlikely to notice the accustomed smells and noises.

However, he'll observe the prisoner, and his interest is similar to that of a visitor: how healthy, strong, emaciated, pale is she? His interest is probably not compassionate, but related to his intentions. A kidnapper needs his victim in good health, while a torturer assesses her capability to suffer and stay alive.

He'll closely listen to the sound of her voice, to detect any note of dejection, despair, rebellion or defiance.

In addition, he'll double-check the security features — the manacles on her wrists, bars on the windows, the door locks.

NOVICE WRITER MISTAKES TO AVOID

Inexperienced writers use only visual descriptions, and miss out the powerful senses of sound, touch and smell.

PROFESSIONAL TIP

Consider making the Black Moment' of your novel a captivity scene. This works especially well in Historical Fiction and Thrillers.

ASSIGNMENT

Write three sentences describing sounds, to insert into different parts of the scene.

Write one sentence each based on the following senses: touch, temperature, smell.

CHAPTER 23

CHASE SCENES

Does your novel-in-progress contain a scene where the main character escapes from danger, with the villain chasing after her? Or perhaps she jumps into a waiting taxi and tells the driver "Follow that car!" Excellent. Readers love these scenes.

Here are some techniques to make your chase scene exciting. I'm using 'she' for the fugitive and 'he' for the pursuer, but of course they can be of any gender.

POINT OF VIEW

Decide whose experience the reader will share: the pursuer's or the fugitive's? Stay in that PoV throughout, showing only what that person sees, hears and feels.

Pursuer's PoV: Focus on the sight of the fleeing person (her back, the way her hair and clothes trail behind her, her running style). Also, show the fleeing person's immediate surroundings (e.g. that she's about to reach a T-junction, or that she's looking for a way to cross that gully). The space between the pursuer and the pursued can also be worth describing briefly in order to show how the distance between them increases or decreases.

Fugitive's PoV: Show what's immediately before her. She will be looking for an escape route, a hiding place or a way to shake off her pursuer, so she'll notice alleyways, rubbish skips, cellar entrances and the like. But she won't pause to think about the architectural styles or the design of the flowerbeds on the way. If the PoV character runs for her life, she won't pause to watch her pursuer, so don't describe what the pursuer looks like, or how the distance between gradually closes. However, you can describe the sounds the pursuer makes: boots thudding on the asphalt, clanking armour, yells, curses.

PACING

Chases are fast paced, so use fast-paced writing techniques: short paragraphs, short sentences, short words. But if the chase or escape spreads over more than a few paragraphs, try to vary the pace. This will make it more exciting. When the PoV character runs fast, use very short sentences — even sentence fragments — and mostly single-syllabic words. They create a sense of breathlessness and fear. When she's hiding, when she's struggling to climb up a facade inch by inch, when the pursuers have trapped her and when the policeman handcuffs her, use medium-length sentences and words.

READER SYMPATHY

Readers tend to sympathise with the fleeing person. If that's your PoV character, you can increase the sympathy effect if several people are hounding the refugee. Nothing stirs reader emotion more than a situation of many against one. If possible, build tension by introducing the other pursuers gradually. At first, she runs only from one foe. Just when she thinks she may get away, one of the villain's henchmen comes from another alley. And then a third. In addition, you can give the pursuer advantages over the refugee: physical health, weapons, technology.

On the other hand, if you want the readers to sympathise with the pursuer, you need to work harder. Emphasise why it is so important that the pursuer catches the fugitive. Perhaps while fleeing, the fugitive does something so ruthless (brutally push a frail old woman out of the way, use a child as a human shield) that the readers will want her stopped. You can also give the fugitive physical or technical advantages (she's a trained athlete with superior stamina, or she drives a faster car), and stack the odds against the pursuer (he has to run with an ankle injury, he drives an old car with faulty steering).

DANGER FROM THE SURROUNDINGS

Increase the tension by shifting the action to increasingly dangerous ground. As your heroine flees from the evil villain, she moves towards quicksand, a crumbling bridge, a cliff edge or a ravine. Now she must decide rapidly which poses the greater danger — pursuer or location — and take the risk. If writing from the pursuer's PoV, let the danger escalate when the pursuer arrives in that spot. For example, the evil fugitive runs across the wobbly wooden bridge, and it starts to collapse behind her. Does the pursuer dare to run across the bridge that's already collapsing?

STUMBLING

When a person runs from danger, a cocktail of chemicals gets released in the brain. It includes adrenalin and other substances which dull pain and give stamina but also impair motor skills. Your fugitive's movements won't be as coordinated as they usually are, so she may miss her footing, stumble or slip. This also applies to the pursuer, although to a lesser extent. The likelihood of tripping is high for both of them, because in their desperate hurry, they won't examine the ground on which they're treading.

PHYSICAL SYMPTOMS

The running characters are probably out of breath, struggling to get enough oxygen. Describe how the PoV character's chest feels like it's about to burst. Her heart thuds loudly, not only in her chest but in her head. This thudding continues even when she stops running, and while she's hiding, the heartbeat in her head may be the loudest noise she hears.

CHASES BY CAR AND ON HORSEBACK

Perhaps the characters chase each other not on foot, but by car (or boat, dog sled, aeroplane), or on horseback (or on donkeys, camels or other animals). In this case, the physical symptoms will be less intense, although the PoV character may still hear her heart drum with excitement or fear. Instead, focus on the noises the vehicles or animals make: screeching tyres, shrieking breaks, panting breath, hooves on asphalt.

Once the pursuer catches up with the fugitive, he'll have to stop her car (or her horse, sled or aeroplane) before he can get at her. Think about how you're going to write that. You may need to ask a professional driver, horse person, pilot or other expert for advice so the action is plausible and authentic.

BYSTANDERS

You can add interest by throwing other people into the action — people who go about their everyday business and are in the way of the fugitive or the pursuers. Don't describe them in detail (your PoV won't take time to observe them), just show how the characters interact with them. For example, your PoV character may upend a market trader's stall in order to block the pursuer's path, or the pursuer may ask, "Which direction did that woman run?" The pursuer may also hurriedly enlist the help of bystanders, e.g. "Stop that thief!" or "Follow that car!"

THE CHASE ENDS IN A FIGHT

When the pursuer catches up with the fugitive, let her put up a fight. This moment is the Climax of the scene, so make it exciting. Don't let the fugitive surrender meekly, or faint. She will struggle one last time before the pursuer overpowers her.

NOVICE WRITER MISTAKES TO AVOID

When penning chase scenes, many inexperienced writers don't go deeply into the PoV's perspective.

PROFESSIONAL TIP

Your MC probably has a special skill, either a natural gift or a knack acquired through experience in a hobby or career. Find a way for him to use this skill to escape his pursuers (or to catch the fugitive).

ASSIGNMENT

Visualise the escape route. Where does the chase begin and end? What obstacles are in the way?

Now imagine the chase as if you were the PoV character, either running for your life or determined to catch the fugitive.

CHAPTER 24

LOVE SCENES

Two people enjoying each other's company in comfortable surroundings, saying "I love you" and feeling happy with not a cloud on the horizon… that's a wonderful experience in real life. But in fiction, it makes a boring love scene. So how do you write a great love scene that rivets your readers and stirs their emotions?

SIX CRUCIAL INGREDIENTS

1. **The scene keeps the characters apart.** I can almost hear you saying "What?! Surely love scenes are about the couple being close?" But if the characters are united in every sense, the scene is static, the love story is over, and the reader is bored. Find a way to keep the characters from being fully united. For example, they may be physically close (holding each other in a tight embrace) but know that they may never meet again. Or perhaps they are with other people, and although they manage to signal their love, they must be careful that nobody else guesses their secret betrothal.

2. **The scene has conflict.** Conflict doesn't mean arguments! Experienced fiction writers know that conflict drives readers to keep reading. A good scene has both inner and outer conflicts.

3. **The scene takes the relationship in a new direction.** Something changes between the two. Perhaps they learn to trust each other more — or maybe the opposite happens, and they trust each other less. They may be more confident about a shared future than before — or their plans for their life together collapse. They are more committed to each other than before — or perhaps one of them withdraws from the commitment.

4. **The scene takes the whole story in a new direction.** Every scene in your book changes the direction of the plot, ideally in ways the reader didn't expect. Twists and turns make the story exciting to read. Love scenes are no exception.

5. **The scene grabs the reader emotionally.** Whether your scene is heart-warming or heart-wrenching, it must do something to the reader's heart. The reader needs to feel what the characters feel — not just love, but the whole mix of emotions the characters go through, such as desire, despair, yearning, hurt, jealousy, trust, gratitude and hope.

6. **The Point-of-View Character grows as a result of the scene.** She will probably be wiser in some way. Perhaps she'll be more cautious or more courageous, bolder or calmer. The other lover who is not the PoV probably changes too, although their growth may be less obvious to the reader.

SAYING "I LOVE YOU"

If your novel contains a love story — either as the main plot or in a sub-plot — there will probably be a moment when one of the characters says "I love you."

This moment is as special for your readers as it is for the characters, so craft it as beautifully as it deserves.

When a character says this, he is committing himself. The moment the words are spoken, the relationship changes.

Delay the moment when those words are spoken. The longer the reader has to wait, the more the emotional tension grows.

Give the character a reason for not saying "I love you" sooner. Here are some ideas. (Let's assume for the moment that it's the man who says it, although in your story it can of course be the woman.)

- He's not certain about his feelings.

- His feelings are inappropriate (e.g. because she belongs to a different class, or is married).

- He worries about her reaction.

- He doesn't want to make himself vulnerable.

- He doesn't want to complicate or ruin a good platonic friendship.

- He doesn't want to burden her with the knowledge of what he feels.

- He doesn't get a chance to talk with her in private.

Why does he say it now? He probably chooses the right time and place. (What makes the time and place right?) On the other hand, he may simply not be able to hold his feelings back any longer.

Insert a sentence of body language before the declaration. This will add meaning and convey emotion:

He cleared his throat. "I love you."

He brushed a finger across her cheek. "I love you."

He clasped her hands in his. "I love you."

What's his body language — is he gazing into her eyes or out of the window? (Let's assume for a moment that it's the male character, though of course it could be the woman.) How does he say it? Describe the tone of his voice — is it tender, deep, hoarse? Does he whisper, stutter, shout?

Does the other person feel the same? Does she return his affections? Does she say "I love you too?"

Perhaps she likes him, or fancies him, but doesn't feel love. In this case, she may say something else nice, either letting him down gently or encouraging him to court her.

If she doesn't want his love, she may pretend not to take it seriously, play it down, or ignore what he said.

Keep the reader in suspense about how the other character will react to the declaration of love. Delay her response. Let her do something before she gives her reply — e.g. arrange the flowers, wipe the wine spill off the table — because this will heighten the suspense and make the moment exciting.

HOW MUCH EROTICISM IS RIGHT FOR YOUR LOVE SCENE?

Some readers enjoy erotic thrills and delight in sharing the characters' intimate moments. Other readers prefer to keep the bedroom door closed. Yet other readers want the relationship to remain unconsummated, but they like to sense the erotic tension building between the two. And many readers want a 'clean' read in which the characters stay chaste.

All these options are 'right' — but not for every novel.

Think carefully about the kind of story you are writing, and the type of readers you are writing it for. Then choose the level of eroticism that's right for the plot and the target audience.

NOVICE WRITER MISTAKES TO AVOID

Inexperienced writers tend to pen love scenes in which both characters are happy, rejoicing in their love and enjoying their togetherness, with no problem or conflict. Don't bore your readers.

Don't write a static love scene in which nothing changes. The scene needs to alter the character, the relationship and the direction of the story.

Many aspiring authors believe that their book will be more successful if they insert sex. However, this is a mistake. Explicit sex can turn away many readers who would otherwise have loved the book. Add erotic action only if it is what your target readers expect.

PROFESSIONAL TIP

When you've written the draft, imagine two other characters acting out the events in this scene and speaking the dialogue.

Does it still work? Then your love scene fails. Scrap it and start again.

A great love scene works only between those two characters, and only at this specific point in their relationship.

FURTHER STUDIES

Writing Love Scenes is a book in the Writer's Craft series. I wrote it with co-author Susanne McCarthy, a Romance novelist.

ASSIGNMENT

Consider the love scene you're planning to write or revise. Does it have all the six vital ingredients? Write down a few notes about how each of these factors apply to the scene.

Do this before you work on the plot, structure and dialogue of the scene.

CHAPTER 25

RELATIONSHIP BREAK-UP SCENES

When lovers break up, they feel intense emotions — whether it's anger or regret, relief or pain. Know what your characters feel, and let the reader feel the same.

If you deal with the break-up in just a few short lines, it won't convince the reader.

Example:

"This is unforgivable. I don't ever want to see you again."

"As you wish. It's over between us."

A reader who sees nothing more than this two-line exchange will expect the couple to calm down and reconcile.

In this chapter we're looking at genuine break-ups.

They deserve a lot more space than a few lines, although the scene may be layered with other plot elements. For example, it could take place while the couple are escaping from the dungeon, scaling a mountain or searching for the lost jewel in the jungle.

Genuine break-ups don't happen on the spur of the moment. At least one of the lovers has thought the matter through. The second character may have seen it coming, or may be taken by surprise.

Even if they part by mutual consent, one of them takes the initiative, while the other reacts. In this chapter, I'll call them the 'upbreaker' and the 'upbreakee' — words I've invented just now.

Who initiates the break-up, and why?

How does the other feel about it?

Why does the upbreaker choose this particular moment to announce the decision?

Does he try to break it to her gently, so as to hurt her as little as possible, or does he want her to suffer?

WHY DO THEY BREAK UP?

Perhaps the two are incompatible. Maybe one has broken the other's trust, and the other cannot forgive this.

The most harrowing situation is a sacrifice: one (or both) of them sacrifice the relationship for something even more important.

The two love each other greatly, and yearn to be together... but something else matters even more, so they sacrifice their love for the greater cause. This is a powerful plot situation especially in Historical Fiction and Epic Fantasy. For example, the queen must marry someone else in order to bring an end to the war and save the lives of her subjects. To make this scene utterly heart-wrenching, let the two lovers agree that the sacrifice is necessary. Their unity in this painful decision shows that they were true soulmates.

Perhaps one character even sacrifices the relationship out of love for the other. This type is rare, but is the most heart-wrenching of them all. The character loves the other person so much that he sets her free. For example, she has a spiritual calling to become a celibate nun. Although they're engaged to be married and he loves her deeply, he understands that she will never be happy unless she follows her religious vocation. So he releases her from the betrothal. Or perhaps she's married to someone else, and will lose her child if she gets divorced. Knowing that her child means more to her than anything else, and that the child depends on its mother, he relinquishes his claim on her.

Readers will shed tears during those scenes, and will never be able to forget your novel.

Depending on the genre you write, the separation doesn't need to be permanent, even though the characters believe that it is. In Romance, circumstances will change so the two will be united for a HEA (Happily-Ever-After) ending.

CONFLICTED FEELINGS

Although the upbreaker knows that she's doing the right thing, and really wants the affair to end, part of her still clings to the relationship. She hopes against hope that things will change in the last minute, and that the break-up can be averted.

This is especially true if they have been together for a long time, if they have planned a future together, or if she loves him intensely.

Example: After eight years as John's mistress, Mary finally realises that he will never leave his wife for her, despite his repeated promises. She wants to end the relationship and make a fresh start. When she tells him it's over, part of her hopes that he'll say, "My wife has agreed to the divorce. We went to see a solicitor this morning. Look, here are the signed documents." Of course she knows this won't happen, but the hope is there.

REFUSING TO ACCEPT

The upbreakee won't simply say "yes, okay" at once, but will react with an emotion — surprise, shock, hurt, humiliation, disbelief — before responding. You can show this emotion with a visceral reaction or with body language.

Then he'll either accept it, or fight for the relationship.

If he accepts, show that it is with a heavy heart, or at least that he is in two minds about it. Write something like this:

He sat staring at his hands for a long time, motionless. Then he faced her. "If this is what you truly want, I won't stand in your way."

More likely, the upbreakee will fight to preserve the relationship, putting forward reasons why they must stay together, and pleading with the upbreaker to give him and their love another chance.

Example: Mary discovered that her boyfriend John has been cheating on her — again. She no longer trusts him and tells him it's over. John pleads with her to give him another chance, promises that this time he'll really stay faithful.

Add a few lines in which the upbreakee pleads for another chance. Together with the upbreaker's own conflicted emotions, this can clench the reader's heart.

EMOTIONS AND BODY LANGUAGE

During a break-up, both characters run through a gamut of emotions.

For a PoV character, you can spell out the emotions, perhaps by showing how it feels physically (visceral responses). For the non-PoV, use facial expression and posture. For both, you can use tone of voice.

Decide on the emotions for each character. Choose at least three, although I recommend five or more.

Here are some suggestions to choose from, although you may add others: regret, resentment, hurt, relief, fear, guilt, embarrassment, shame, anger, hatred, longing, despair, pity, hope, humiliation, triumph.

Some emotions will be present throughout the scene, others will come and go.

For example, a character may feel guilt, then pity, then relief. Or he may feel anger at first, then confusion and disbelief, and finally humiliation and hurt.

The characters may not admit those emotions openly, but may try to hide or suppress them.

AFTER THE BREAK-UP

If you use the 'scene & sequel' format of scene structure, the sequel should be filled with the PoV character's emotions, showing how she feels after the break-up. Instead of spelling them out, describe them viscerally: *Hollow pain ached in her chest where love and hope used to be.*

She may tell herself that she's done the right thing, that it's wonderful to be free, that she can now make a new start. Or she may plot how to get the man back.

NOVICE WRITER MISTAKES TO AVOID

Don't deal with the break-up in a few quick lines, and don't skimp on emotions.

PROFESSIONAL TIP

Make the break-up as difficult as possible for the PoV character. The reason for the difficulty can be whatever suits the story — love, guilt or fear. Just don't make it easy.

FURTHER READING

Other chapters in the book *Writing Love Scenes* (co-written by me and Romance novelist Suzanne McCarthy) may be helpful.

ASSIGNMENT

Make a list of the emotions each character feels — both the PoV and the other. For each emotion, think of at least one way to convey this to the reader, for example, a body language clue, a visceral reaction, or a dialogue sentence.

CHAPTER 26

EROTIC SCENES

Does your novel have an erotic scene, where the lovers share intimate joys? Here are some guidelines to help you craft this section so it enchants your readers.

GET THE HEAT LEVEL RIGHT

Some novels are 'clean reads' in which the characters stay chaste, with minimal erotic tension and no erotic action. Others sizzle with erotic tension and passionate kisses, while yet others seek to arouse readers by sharing explicit action.

Which is right for your novel? You need to decide the 'heat level' before you even start to plot the scene. It must be right for your story and your intended readers. Especially in the Romance genre, readers know what they like, and they select novels which deliver the heat level of their personal preference.

If you're writing a 'clean read', you don't need to read on. But if you want your fiction to sizzle and steam, these tips can help.

USE THE SENSES

You can make your readers receptive to erotic action by activating their senses. Use sensory descriptions of not just what the PoV character sees, but what she hears, smells, touches and more. This applies to everything around the couple as well as to the lover's body.

How many senses are there? People often talk about 'the five senses' (seeing, hearing, smelling, tasting, touching) but actually there are many more. Aim to use at least four.

Let's look at some of them, and at how you can use them in your erotic scene.

Seeing

Focus on detail. Describe the plump juiciness of the strawberry instead of the whole content of the fruit bowl, and the dark hairs above the waistband of his boxers rather than an overall impression of his body hair. Describe colours and shapes imaginatively, perhaps using similes.

Here's a professional technique you may want to try: take an unattractive feature of the lover's appearance and describe it in an appealing way. For example, when they first met, his heavily scarred face may have looked unattractive to her, but in this scene, every ridge and furrow strikes her as handsome. Describing something unattractive in attractive terms takes advanced writing skills. Try it: the results will give the scene extra power.

Hearing

Near the beginning of the scene, describe gentle sounds from the surroundings — the hum of insects in the meadow, the crackling of the fire in the chimney, the tapping of raindrops against the window pane. Describe how the lover's voice and breath sound.

Smelling

This is the most powerful sense, the one that will activate your readers' subconscious the most.

The best time to describe the smells is when the Point-of-View character enters a new location. The moment she enters the room, mention the scent of wood smoke from the open fireplace, and when the couple walk into the forest, mention the aromas of pine resin and earthy moss. When they go to bed, that's the time to give the reader a whiff of the lavender-scented sheets.

As the couple get closer, describe the smell of the partner's body, e.g. he may smell of leather, lemony cologne and fresh male sweat.

Important: In an erotic scene, evoke only pleasant aromas. Any unpleasant odour would put the reader off.

Tasting

Are the lovers sharing a meal or a drink at the beginning of the scene? Describe the flavours. Perhaps the couple's intimate activities involve food and drink, too — she could feed him strawberries, or he may lick whipped cream out of her navel.

Naturally, you can also describe the taste of the lover's skin and more... but I'll leave those details to your (and your characters') imagination.

Touching

This sense matters more in erotic scenes than in any other kind of fiction.

Begin by describing what it feels like when the point-of-view character touches objects: the velvety skin of the peach, the slippery smoothness of the satin bedsheets. Describe what it feels like when her bare feet walk across the fluffy carpet, the wooden planks or the freshly mown grass. These descriptions awaken the senses and prepare your readers for intimate touches.

When the lovers get physical, describe how the partner's skin, hair, lips and breath feel.

Temperature

This is one of the less-known senses, and sometimes lumped together with touching (something feels cold or warm to the touch) or with tasting (the drink feels cool or hot on the tongue).

However, it's worth paying attention to this sense, especially in an erotic scene, where the temperature can play a major role. The chilly weather outside or the unheated room can motivate the characters to huddle closely together for warmth. You can describe the cosy heat emanating from the log fire, the hot sand under her bare soles, the lovely cool breeze caressing her skin, the cool prickle of the champagne bubbling on the tongue, or the sheets feeling cold when she crawls into bed but pleasantly warm on the side where he has lain a moment ago.

Describe the partner's temperature. Is his body warmer or colder than hers? Do his fingers feel cool or hot on her skin? How about his breath?

MAKE IT UNIQUE

Craft the scene so it could unfold only between those two specific characters, and only at this point in their relationship.

If other characters could act out the same scene, then it's too generic. Start over. Their way of lovemaking should arise from the characters' individual personalities, past experiences, hopes, fears and desires.

The same applies if you could move the scene to much earlier or much later in the book. Their lovemaking needs to reflect how their relationship and attitudes have developed. If you could move a scene to a different section of the novel requiring only minimal changes, the scene is not good enough.

CONSENT

Before the couple have sex, make sure they both give their consent. Your readers will feel better if there is no room for doubt.

In 1970s romance novels, the heroine sometimes said "no" but he knew that she really meant "yes" and proceeded. And sometimes he took her by force against her will, to demonstrate what a masterful man he was, and her cries of protest turned into moans of lust. Today's readers would find this behaviour unacceptable.

To ensure that your readers know that the characters have given full consent, add a little dialogue. One can ask "Are you sure you want this?" and the other replies, "Yes. Oh, yes please." Then you're safe, and your readers will relax and enjoy themselves.

LANGUAGE

Readers may giggle if you use archaic words, or get overly metaphorical in order to avoid naming body parts. Try to get it right for your readers. There is no single 'right' language. What feels natural to some readers is shocking to others, and what some find silly, others may find arousing.

Write it so it's right for the kind of readers who you want to read your book. Do those readers prefer to read about his penis, his member, his shaft, his tool, his cock, his dick or his manhood?

If you're unsure what language to choose, study the recent bestselling novels in your subgenre. Those are the kind of novels your target readers enjoy. Model your word choices on those examples.

NOVICE WRITER MISTAKES TO AVOID

Many new authors insert graphic sex in the mistaken belief that this will make their book more marketable or more popular. But unless the sex scene is appropriate for the book and the intended audience, it will alienate readers.

PROFESSIONAL TIP

At the end of the scene, show how the relationship between the two characters has been affected by the intimacy.

How? Perhaps they like each other more now... but perhaps they like each other less. Maybe they've fallen in love... or maybe they used to be in love, and now feel that it was a mistake. Do they trust each other more now that they've shared such intimacy... or less?

You can create interesting conflicts and complications if the change is one-sided, or if their attitudes have changed in opposite directions. What if he now respects her more than before... but she respects him less? What if she finally trusts him... but he no longer trusts her?

(This tip doesn't apply to the Porn genre which rarely shows much character development.)

FURTHER STUDIES

In *Writing Love Scenes,* my co-author Susanne McCarthy shares many tips about how to create erotic tension and write about sex.

ASSIGNMENT

Write a sentence describing, from the PoV character's perspective, how the lover smells.

CHAPTER 27

DUEL SCENES

A duel adds excitement, action and drama to a novel. Could it fit with your plot?

Historical novels (including Westerns and Historical Romance) are often a natural fit, but other genres (like Fantasy and Science Fiction) can lend themselves, too.

A duel is a fight between two people, with pre-agreed rules. Both parties agree to fight each other, and they agree to the rules, the location and the weapons. Sometimes, a duel is arranged on the spur of the moment, for example, when two cowboys in a saloon quarrel about cheating at cards and decide to step out into the street to shoot it out. Other duels may be arranged hours or days in advance, for instance, two gentlemen of the Regency period say they'll settle the matter of a lady's honour behind the church at dawn.

Duels are almost always about matters of honour. The person who feels offended in their honour — or who considers his woman's or his family's honour insulted — demands 'satisfaction', that is, he challenges the other to a duel.

Refusing a challenge would brand a person as a coward. However, the person who has been challenged usually gets the right to choose the place, the time and the weapon, which gives him some advantage.

Duellists are usually young men from the upper classes. In some societies and historical periods, duelling was so epidemic that it was the most frequent cause of death among young men. Only members of the same social class duelled; it was considered dishonourable to duel someone of lower status, and low-ranking people didn't have the right to challenge their betters.

Duelling is usually armed combat, and any type of weapon is possible. The most frequently used weapons are fencing swords (such as rapiers) and handguns, but the duellists might also fight with cricket bats, pitchforks, poisonous snakes or any other usual or unusual arms.

Before the fight, the duellists agree on rules. In a society where duels are common, they may agree to follow the established rules. Otherwise, they create their own. Both combatants behave with utmost courtesy and consideration, even if they hate each other's guts.

A fight may be 'to the death' (the survivor wins) or 'first blood' (the duel is over when one of them is wounded; the uninjured fighter wins). If the duel is to the death, each may promise to support the other's widow and orphans.

If the duel is fought about matters of honour, the duel erases the dishonour. Whoever survives — whether one or both — is not supposed to bring the matter up again.

Readers like fair fighting in duel scenes, especially when the hero and the villain outdo each other with polite fairness.

Duelling — at least duelling to the death — is mostly a male thing, apparently wired into the male psychology. In some periods, young men seemed to feel the need to prove their masculinity by duelling. Women don't seem to feel the need to prove their femininity this way. Bear this psychological difference in mind, although you can of course use female duellists if it suits your characters, society and plot.

Each duellist may invite an assistant, called a 'second'. The two seconds act as referees and as witnesses. They also carry messages, measure out the distance for the shooting, and check that everything is fair. You can create interesting plot situations if the duellists are scrupulously fair, but one of the seconds is cheating.

There may also be a doctor or healer, a referee or a judge present.

In the case of 'trial by combat' — a legal dispute decided by fighting — there'll also be an officer of the law, a priest, and a representative of the ruler.

If the law forbids duelling, the victor may face a charge of murder. To prevent this, the duellists and their seconds may create a situation so precisely timed that the witnesses can testify that both duellists acted in simultaneous self-defence.

TIPS FOR WRITING YOUR DUEL SCENE

- If writing historical fiction, research the following: Was duelling legal at the time? This determines whether the combatants fight publicly or in secret with only selected witnesses. What was society's attitude to duels? Duelling might be forbidden by law, but admired by society. If a man's reputation depends on having fought in a duel, young males will be quick to challenge one another. What weapons were used at the time?

- In the first half of the novel, your main character may wound or kill a minor character who is no longer needed for the plot. A duel in the middle of the novel often pitches the MC against another important good character (such as the heroine's beloved brother) which creates drama and tragedy. The novel's climax is a good place for a fight to the death between the MC and the villain.

- Stack the odds against the character for whom you want the reader to root. For example, if the fight is between the hero and the villain, make the hero a decent swordsman, but the villain a famed fencing champion who has never been defeated.

- Choose the location carefully. Decide whether it is public or private. Duellists may decide to fight away from the eye of the law, or in a place where bullets won't accidentally hurt bystanders. On the other hand, they may choose to fight where they have the biggest possible audience. Normally, they will select level, secure ground, but they may choose the added danger of fighting on a rope bridge over an abyss or a frozen lake surface.

- Consider how the setting affects the fight. How even and firm is the ground? Who has the sun in his eyes, the wind at his back?

- Use the weather to add atmosphere and complications. How does the persistent drizzle, sudden downpour, hazy mist, thick fog, extreme heat, blowing wind or frozen-over ground affect the visuals and the action?

- Let both combatants act with scrupulous fairness. This gives the duel a poignancy readers love. A cheating villain would devalue the duel scene in the reader's eyes.

- Put dialogue before the beginning of the fight. The duellists and their seconds may formally agree to rules and make last-minute arrangements and promise to protect their dead rival's orphans. They may trade insults, although it is more likely (and more effective) if they talk with utmost courtesy to the man they plan to kill. It is also possible that the seconds, a bystander or one of the duellists makes a final attempt to avert the fight.

- Real life duels are short and over quickly, but readers enjoy a drawn-out fight in which the characters display their skills, especially with sword fights. Flesh out the fight scene and satisfy your readers. Find a way to establish earlier in the novel how skilled the fighters are, so the feats during the duel feel plausible.

- Once the fight is under way, use short paragraphs, short sentences and short words. This conveys a sense of fast, breathless pacing.

- Let the reader hear the sounds of the fight: zinging bullets, clanking swords, panting breaths. Sounds create excitement.

- After the fight, show the damage — the dead body, the wounds. This gives the scene realism, poignancy and emotion. Depending on the genre, you may want to describe the gory details in full, or give just a quick glimpse of red blood staining the fallen foe's shirt.

DUEL SCENES WORTH STUDYING

If you can, watch the final duel in the movie *Rob Roy* — it's a perfect example. You may find it on YouTube by searching 'Rob Roy Duel'. Make sure you view the full excerpt starting where the combatants pick up the swords, and see how the suspense builds as they agree formally to the terms.

The movie *Troy* shows a duel that's been famous for thousands of years. On YouTube, you can search for 'Troy Duel Achilles Hector'.

The duel in *Sanjuro* is famous for its realism and speed. Search for 'Sanjuro Duel'. Watch the scene from the start, to see how one combatant tries to talk the other out of fighting. Once the fight begins, it's over fast — so fast that it leaves the viewer stunned. For most fiction scenarios, this is too quick, but it's nevertheless worth watching.

NOVICE WRITER MISTAKES TO AVOID

Don't use dialogue while the opponents are fighting. They won't have the breath to spare, and they're focused on the action. Conversations during the action make the fight unrealistic.

PROFESSIONAL TIP

Insert dialogue immediately before the start of the duel. Depending on the situation, the opponents may hurl accusations, taunt each other, politely agree on terms, or honourably promise to take care of the other's orphans. This will also show their personality.

FURTHER STUDIES

My book *Writing Fight Scenes* contains a wealth of useful information and advice you can use in duel scenes, from weapons to word choices.

ASSIGNMENT

Write a sentence from the actual fight. Pick a moment when the action is in full swing, and one character shoots or strikes the other. Focus on the physical experience of hitting/shooting/whatever, and use vivid verbs.

CHAPTER 28

BATTLE SCENES

When the plot calls for a battle — for example, in a Historical Romance novel — many writers are at a loss as to how to craft this scene.

Some skip the challenge altogether, flash forward to the next scene, and deprive the readers of the experience. (*When Konrad returned with his victorious army...*) However, disappointing your readers is not a good option.

Others authors grit their teeth and pen the scene, but find it a struggle, and their beta readers and editors tell them that this part does not match the quality of the rest of the book.

Let's look at how you can write a plausible, exciting battle scene.

YOUR BATTLE STRATEGY

1. Choose the PoV carefully, and stick with it. The individual fighter has to be totally focused on the action affecting him. This is a very limited view. He can't see what goes on a few feet from him, let alone what's happening at the other end of the battlefield or how the sun dyes the horizon bloody red. Resist the temptation to provide a 'big picture' view while the fighting is on.

2. Provide the reader with 'big picture' information before and after the battle. Before the battle begins, you can show the terrain, the size of the enemy army, and other aspects you want the reader to know. When the battle is over, the reader can see the outcome: which side won, how many have fallen, who has survived.

3. Stack the odds against your heroes. The readers' natural sympathies lie with the smaller army. The greater you can make

the numerical difference, the better. The evil overlord's army is bigger than the hero's, and it is much better equipped, too.

4. Battles don't just happen: they are planned. At least one side seeks the battle and is prepared. While there have been occasions in history when enemy units bumped into each other by accident and started fighting, this is not the norm, and unless you're very knowledgeable about military matters, it won't come across as plausible.

5. The generals plan a battle strategy in advance, and make sure that their officers know it. In the heat of the battle, it's often impossible to change strategy or give orders. Sometimes, soldiers are still fighting when the battle has already been decided, because they don't know that their king is dead or the enemy general has surrendered.

6. Often, the location decides the outcome of the battle. Generals choose the location carefully — and so should you, the author!

    If the battle takes place on a slope, the army uphill has a huge advantage, because it's easier to fight downhill than uphill, and because missiles fly further.

    Each general tries to make the battle happen in terrain which favours his own army, and where the enemy can't fully deploy his. For example, chariots are fearsome on the plain, but useless in the mountains. Foot archers can fight on any terrain, especially in the mountains. The general who has many chariots will try to force a battle on the plain, while the general who has archers will try to lure his enemy into mountainous terrain.

    If one general has a small army and his enemy has a large one, he'll try to lure them into a gorge or other restricted space where they can't move.

7. Armies are organised in units either by level of skill and experience (elite, veterans, novices, untrained peasants...) or by

weapons and equipment (cavalry, infantry, archers, spearmen, chariots...) or both. To which unit does your PoV character belong?

8. Before the battle, the general probably addresses the troops, firing their fighting spirit and courage.

   This pep talk may include depersonalising the enemy, because soldiers are more willing to kill monsters than to kill fellow human beings. It's easy to kill a man whom you consider a menace to your children, and difficult to kill him if you think of him as a fellow human who loves his children as much as you love yours.

   (The pep talk may or may not be part of this scene).

9. While the fight is on, the PoV character is totally focused on two things: to survive and to kill. He won't see anything or anyone other than the enemy soldier opposite him.

10. The PoV may get injured, and depending on the nature of the wound, he may fight on. If he stops, he'll get killed. The real pain may not kick in until after the fight when the adrenaline wears off.

11. Noble emotions and ideals have no room during a battle. The thinker of noble thoughts and carrier of high ideals during a battle won't survive. If you want to show your hero's nobility, do it when the fighting is over, for example, in his treatment of surviving enemies.

12. Consider using interesting or extreme weather to make your battle scene unusual. Imagine pristine snow which gets trampled, becomes slippery, and stains red with blood. Or a strong wind which blows arrows off course. Or blistering heat and glaring sun. Or week-long rain turning the field into knee-deep mud, making it difficult for foot soldiers, let alone horses or chariots. Or fog blocking the view of the enemy.

HOW TO STRUCTURE A BATTLE SCENE

Part 1: Suspense

Describe the terrain, convey the battle strategy, show the preparations. The general gives a pep talk, the soldiers ready their weapons, say their prayers, get into position.

Part 2: Start

Both armies shoot missiles (bullets, cannon balls, stones or arrows) to take out as many of the enemy as possible before they get close. In a Historical novel, clouds of arrows may darken the sky before the battle begins.

Part 3: Action

The PoV fights. Everything happens very fast, so use fast-paced techniques, such as short sentences, short words, lots of verbs, few adjectives, no adverbs. Keep to the PoV's narrow range of awareness.

Part 4 (optional): Surprise

Something unexpected happens and changes the course of the battle. Perhaps a relief force arrives to support one army, or a sudden downpour turns the ground into mud. Use this optional part only if your battle scene is long and detailed.

Part 5: Climax

This is the most exciting section of the fight scene. Make it fast-paced, breathless, dangerous. The challenge for the writer lies in shaping this part as the Climax of the battle although the PoV character isn't aware that it's the Climax. If possible, arrange it so your hero kills an important enemy personage, maybe their general, or their most fearsome warrior. This may not reflect the reality of most battles, but it pleases the readers.

Part 6: Aftermath

This section is also where you reveal the overall outcome of the battle. The PoV character and his comrades bandage their wounds and mourn their dead.

This is where you can inject realism if it suits your genre. Soon after the battle, there'll be carrion birds (e.g. crows, vultures) feeding on the corpses. There'll be humans (probably the victorious soldiers) gathering up reusable weapons (because weapons are valuable) and looting the corpses. The battlefield is covered in blood, gore, and amputated limbs. The stench is awful, because in death, the bladder and bowels have opened. Plus, there's the smell from injuries, not just blood (which starts to stink only after a while) but the content of stomachs and intestines from belly wounds. The stench gets worse after a few hours, especially if the weather is hot. After some hours, the corpses will be crawling with flies, and before long, there'll be maggots.

Obviously, in a Romance novel you'll want to tone down the gruesome bits, while in an Action novel you may want to play them up.

NOVICE WRITER MISTAKES TO AVOID

Inexperienced writers allow their soldier character to observe what his mates are doing at the other side of the battlefield and how the sun sets on the horizon, and to think about life, death, politics and other matters while he's fighting. This is not realistic. If a soldier took his attention off the immediate fight for even a moment, he'd be dead.

PROFESSIONAL TIP

Provide a description of the terrain and any other information the reader needs in the build-up before the actual fight starts. The section immediately before the battle is often a natural place for this, because the soldier will observe these facts at this stage.

FURTHER STUDY

My book *Writing Fight Scenes* contains detailed advice on all kinds of fighting, weapons, battle strategy and more.

ASSIGNMENT

Write a sentence in which the PoV character is exhausted (and possibly injured) but fights on. Focus on the physical effort it takes to lift that gun, swing that sword, do whatever he must to survive.

DEAR READER,

I hope you found these tips helpful and can implement them for many scenes you are working on now and will be crafting in the future. Remember: my suggestions are tools, and you choose how to apply them in your writing.

I'll be delighted if you post a review on Amazon or some other book site where you have an account and posting privileges. Maybe you can mention what kind of fiction you write, and explain which chapters you found most helpful and why.

Email me the link to your review, and I'll send you a free review copy (ebook) of one of my other Writer's Craft books. Let me know which one you would like: *Writing Fight Scenes, Writing Scary Scenes, The Word-Loss Diet, Writing About Magic, Writing About Villains, Writing Dark Stories, Euphonics For Writers, Writing Short Stories to Promote Your Novels, Twitter for Writers, Why Does My Book Not Sell? 20 Simple Fixes, Writing Vivid Settings, How To Train Your Cat To Promote Your Book, Writing Deep Point of View, Getting Book Reviews, Novel Revision Prompts, Writing Vivid Dialogue, Writing Vivid Characters, Writing Book Blurbs and Synopses, Writing Vivid Plots, Write Your Way Out Of Depression: Practical Self-Therapy For Creative Writers, Fantasy Writing Prompts, Horror Writing Prompts, Dr Rayne's Guide to Writerly Disorders, Writing Love Scenes.*

In some chapters, I've made suggestions for further study. You may want to choose one of those books for your review.

My email is <u>contact@raynehall.com</u>. Drop me a line if you've spotted any typos which have escaped the proof-reader's eagle eyes, or want to give me private feedback or have questions.

You can also contact me on Twitter: <u>https://twitter.com/RayneHall</u>. Tweet me that you've read this book, and I'll probably follow you back.

If you find this book helpful, it would be great if you could spread the word about it. Maybe you know other writers who would benefit.

With best wishes for your writing success,

Rayne Hall

ACKNOWLEDGEMENTS

I give sincere thanks to the beta readers and critiquers who read the draft chapters and offered valuable feedback: Amanda Jakle, Melissa Tacket, Suzan St Maur, Lin White, Alex Binkley, MK Goodwin, Clare Dale, Jake TS Wryte.

The book cover is by Erica Syverson and Manuel Berbin. Jonathan Broughton proofread the manuscript, and Eled Cernik formatted the book.

My cats Sulu and Yura took turns snuggling on the desk between my arms as I typed — the perfect writing muses: approving, encouraging and sweet. The third cat, Janice, 'helped' in different ways. The little rascal often jumped on the keyboard to type into the manuscript. She has a distinctive writing style ("ww44444444444445 bn") and I hope that the beta readers, the proofreader and I have caught all her creative additions.

Rayne Hall

Made in the USA
Coppell, TX
09 May 2022

77595165R00079